Enlightenment Through the Path of Kundalini

A Guide to a Positive Spiritual Awakening and Overcoming Kundalini Syndrome

Tara Springett

© Copyright by Tara Springett 2014
All rights reserved
ISBN-13: 978-1506067612
ISBN-10: 1506067611

Contents

Introduction 5

Kundalini and Enlightenment 11

How we Change Through a Kundalini Awakening 31

Preparation for Awakening the Kundalini 61

Purification of the Chakras 79

Awakening the Kundalini 114

Dealing with the Challenges of a Kundalini Awakening 141

The Deity-State 187

Appendix - Testimonials for Kundalini Healing 205

About Tara Springett 209

Acknowledgements

My deepest thank you goes to my Buddhist teacher Rigdzin Shikpo who helped me to direct my life in such a rewarding direction.

Garchen Rinpoche, my deepest gratitude goes to you for facilitating a fresh influx of kundalini in 2001.

Nigel, my soulmate and husband – I cannot say thank you enough for supporting and accompanying me in my kundalini process, for discussing every single line of this book with me and for editing it. Most of all, I am grateful that you are willing to walk the spiritual path together.

Most gratitude must go to my heavenly mother White Tara who spoke to me and gave me the knowledge to understand the kundalini and spiritual development and, in that way, enabled me to help others.

Introduction

This book is written for everyone who wants to learn about the mysterious phenomenon of kundalini and use it to reach the pinnacle of human development - enlightenment. The book is also for those who are going through an involuntary awakening and seeking help to alleviate their symptoms and make the best of this event.

I have been treating clients who had an involuntary kundalini awakening for a number of years and I know that this can be scary. The last thing these people want is more 'horror stories' about the kundalini. And I can reassure you right here that this will not be another book full of scary stories about the kundalini but a guide that will help you to understand what is happening to you and to recognise it for what it is: a positive event that will urge you to live a healthier and more spiritual life.

For both kinds of people – those who are seeking a safe awakening of the kundalini and those who are looking for help after an involuntary awakening - this book will show you how to use the kundalini to develop towards enlightenment in leaps and bounds. You will learn that kundalini is like the fuel that will carry the vehicle of your body and mind towards your highest potential of love, wisdom and bliss.

If you have not yet had a kundalini awakening, I will show you a pathway of awakening that is extraordinarily safe, so that you can use this wonderful energy to further and enrich your spiritual life. The path I will be teaching is slow but you will feel its benefits pretty much from day one.

My own kundalini was roughly awakened through a year of bio-energetic therapy in which I participated at the age of 24. It was a rather disturbing experience that propelled me into a deep crisis. Yet now, almost 30 years later, I feel it was one of the best things that ever happened to me because it greatly accelerated my spiritual and personal development in every way.

I wish that my awakening had happened more gently and with a knowledgeable guide at my side so that the initial impact had been less confusing and painful. But the long-term effects of my kundalini awakening were nothing less than wonderful. Throughout the intervening 30 years, I have undergone tremendous and positive changes in every aspect of my life that were all initiated within me through my kundalini awakening all those years ago. There were also a number of challenges along the way that I had to master all by myself because, for many years, I did not even know what had happened to me. Back then, I did not have the Internet to help me self-diagnose what was going on within me.

After my initial awakening it was not long before I started to harvest the enormous blessings of this extraordinary event: a deep sense of meaning and purpose and the feeling that everything in my life served the one overarching goal of reaching enlightenment for the sake of all beings.

It was only a year after my kundalini first rose that I started to immerse myself into Tibetan Buddhist meditation and have done so ever since. Over the years I also developed my professional life as a psychotherapist and found my own challenges very useful as they enabled me to have more empathy for my clients and to help them more efficiently. In 1997 my Buddhist teachers asked me to work as a Buddhist teacher - giving me the opportunity to help others to progress on their own spiritual path.

Due to the kundalini circulating in my system, I became more and more clairvoyant and this heightened awareness was very useful in helping my clients and myself faster. I also experienced rushes of creativity that led to the discovery of the psycho-spiritual method of higher-consciousness healing in 1998. This transpersonal approach to healing proved highly efficient and has helped hundreds - even thousands - of people to free themselves from the most debilitating problems, including all kundalini symptoms.

Yet, even at that time I did not realise that much of my own development was due to a kundalini awakening. This was to change when in 2002 I asked my Buddhist teacher Garchen Rinpoche to initiate me into the Tibetan Buddhist meditation of 'tummo', which is the Tibetan Buddhist equivalent of a kundalini awakening practice. I was very interested in this initiation as it is clearly stated in the Tibetan Buddhist system that tummo is the prerequisite for all higher stages of mind and especially enlightenment.

Garchen Rinpoche initiated me willingly and he also teaches the basics of a kundalini awakening publicly and in his books. Usually, the kundalini practice of tummo is not taught publicly in Tibetan Buddhism because it can be abused for egotistical purposes and it can also cause difficult side effects. However, times have changed and other Tibetan Buddhist teachers have also started to teach this practice publicly, as well. Most noteworthy are Lama Yeshe in his book 'The Bliss of Inner Fire' and Geshe Kelsang Gyatso in his book 'Clear Light of Bliss'.

Once I had my tummo initiation, I started to research every available book about tummo and kundalini and it was only then that it slowly dawned on me that I had already had a kundalini awakening back in 1984. Under the guidance of Garchen Rinpoche my experience became a lot more rewarding and I started to experience more and more unconditional happiness and bliss coursing through my inner being in undulating waves of ecstasy.

For a long time I thought that I should never teach how to awaken the kundalini because it can be abused for egotistical purposes and there can also be a number of challenges during this process. I myself experienced these problems only to a small degree but I know many people who suffered more than I ever have. Therefore, for many years I stuck to what I did best: helping my psychotherapy clients and meditation students to overcome emotional and relationship-related problems by teaching self-awareness and loving kindness towards themselves and others.

However, after I was into my own kundalini awakening for almost 20 years I received yet another wonderful blessing: I became able to directly communicate with my higher power, the Tibetan Buddhist deity White Tara.

At first it happened in a very subtle way and I simply felt I received answers to my prayers around my daily life issues. These were very precise predictions about what would happen, for example, with some problems we faced when bringing up our son and while trying to buy a house. Soon I began to write down these 'answers' I received in meditation and kept a very critical eye on whether or not these predictions came true. To my great astonishment they virtually all came true – even in the most unlikely cases - and this has continued to happen over the course of more than ten years.

I had tried predictive methods many times before, like working with a pendulum or using Tarot cards. My results were usually very unreliable and it never took long before I gave up on these methods as I felt I was confusing myself unnecessarily. But once I tried to communicate with White Tara directly, these 'errors' just did not reoccur. Throughout the last ten years I have asked many questions around matters concerning my family and myself and overall I have found this way of working to be highly accurate.

After working in this way for one or two years, I started to ask White Tara numerous questions about spiritual development. I asked these questions randomly and only transferred them afterwards into an ordered manuscript. All in all, I assembled a book of 250 pages filled with the most condensed bullet points about every aspect of spiritual development from kundalini to chakras and from manifesting to enlightenment.

Many bits of information that I received from White Tara during my sessions challenged my own views and forced me to ask numerous additional questions to actually understand what she was trying to say. Sometimes I kept asking the same questions over and over until I was finally able to assimilate the information into my own understanding.

Slowly, a cohesive structure of spiritual teachings emerged that was free of any internal contradictions, even though I had asked White Tara many hundreds of questions about a wide variety of topics and often found her answers rather confusing at first.

One may ask why I tried to channel all these questions instead of going to a learned Buddhist teacher or trying to find the answers in the Buddhist literature. My problem was that I wanted to find out about the finer points of very advanced teachings (like kundalini, for example) and these topics are usually not publicly taught in Tibetan Buddhism. The few books that are written about these themes are not easy to understand as in Tibetan Buddhism the real meaning of highly esoteric topics is often kept secret by the use of cryptic language that needs to be interpreted by a knowledgeable teacher. The last option of asking all my questions in private interviews with my teacher was also impossible as Tibetan Buddhist lamas are usually flooded with students and have no time for someone like me who yearns for hundreds of hours of teaching.

That is the reason why I turned to channelling White Tara directly. Despite the fact that I often found it difficult to understand her lessons at first, I compared them with what I had learnt from my teachers and the Buddhist literature and I believe that they are in line with the official Buddhist teachings. Therefore, I would like to offer you these teachings in the best faith and with the motivation to benefit you in your spiritual journey by giving you teachings that are otherwise hard to come by. Any faults are entirely my own.

For the learned Buddhist scholars among my readers I would like to point out that White Tara did not use Buddhist terminology in my channelling sessions. Instead she used English words, which I understood to be equivalents of the Sanskrit and Tibetan terms. I very much liked these words or word creations because they were more self-explanatory than their foreign scholarly counterparts. In addition, White Tara used psychological and scientific terms that suited my own background in psychotherapy but cannot be found in the Buddhist literature.

I have sprinkled numerous passages that I have channelled directly from White Tara throughout this book. If it appears to you that these passages are similar in structure and wording to my own writing, then please do not discount them as my own inventions. I have done all my channelling in a process called automatic writing in which I put a pen to the paper and 'let it write on its own'. The outcome of this technique was texts that were often grammatically incorrect but full of amazing concepts, interesting metaphors and word creations that were genuinely new and unknown to me.

As I said before, I never thought I should teach these advanced esoteric teachings that White Tara taught me but from a certain point onwards she started to urge me to do just that. She said that she wanted me to write several books about the material she had given to me and that I should start with a book about kundalini.

For years I was highly reluctant to fulfil White Tara's request and used every excuse to avoid this task. Simply put, I was not confident enough to stand before the world and declare that I had channelled material from White Tara because I feared ridicule, rejection and criticism. But while I was refusing to do this task, my own life became more and more difficult and I experienced every possible rejection in my professional life until I felt almost heart-broken.

Eventually, I told myself that if I read about someone who was refusing a 'divine order' to write a book, I would think that this person was a fool. So, with a mighty 'getting over myself', I am here to bring to you what White Tara has given to me. I also feel that I owe it to the increasing numbers of clients who see me about kundalini problems to write down what I have learnt about kundalini so that they can find a way to alleviate their suffering more quickly and receive the full blessing of their awakening.

For years, I have used what I learnt during my channelling sessions with White Tara with my clients and overall the results are very encouraging. Using these teachings in conjunction with the higher-consciousness healing technique, I was able to help numerous clients who were confused by their involuntary kundalini awakening and suffered from a number of symptoms. They all became dramatically better within a few months.

In this book I will outline White Tara's step-by-step approach to safely awaken your kundalini so that you can advance more quickly on your spiritual path. In the last chapter I will explain to you what White Tara taught me about reaching enlightenment by using your kundalini and merging with your higher power.

The path of awakening outlined in this book is extremely safe but I would like to say as a disclaimer that awakening kundalini is only safe for the sincere spiritual student who is deeply motivated to use these teachings solely for the sake of all sentient beings. In an ideal world, you should also have an experienced spiritual guide who can support you along the way.

Who is White Tara?

White Tara is a very popular goddess in Tibetan Buddhism. Her Tibetan name is Drolma which means 'she who saves'. White Tara is the Tibetan equivalent of the Hindu goddess Parvati and the Chinese deity Kwan Yin.

White Tara is the deity for overcoming obstacles and long life. She looks white in colour, has two arms and so-called 'wisdom eyes' in the soles of her feet, in the palms of her hands and in the centre of her forehead. People pray to her for help with everyday problems and for guidance on their spiritual path.

Now is the time to let White Tara speak 'directly' to you. In one of my channelling sessions I asked her who she is and this is what she 'told' me:

> *I am the force who is behind all phenomena in the world. I am the love that alleviates all pain and the joy that brings happiness wherever there is suffering. I am the power that holds the universes together and the energy that makes the sun shine and the stars rotate on their pathways through the sky. I am the power that you can trust and I am the help you have always been seeking. I am your true home, your alpha and omega, your goal and destination.*

When I read these words it sends shivers up my spine and tears to my eyes. For me, her words are certainly true but it is important to understand that White Tara is just one emanation of countless deities or divine principle that appears in all sorts of forms and figures in every genuine spiritual path around the globe. Whether you believe in the Christian God, in another Buddhist deity or simply in an angelic figure, the only thing that matters is that you have faith that your higher power is the source of deepest love and wisdom in the universe. No one needs to convert to Buddhism or to the worship of White Tara. Instead, I encourage you to use White Tara's teachings to go more deeply into your own spiritual path.

Chapter One
Kundalini and Enlightenment

According to Tibetan Buddhism, enlightenment is more than a blissful feeling. It is actually the discovery of our own divinity, which is pure love and wisdom together with numerous supernatural powers. In order to reach this state we need to awaken a certain energy within us called 'tummo' in Tibetan Buddhism but more commonly known as kundalini.

The word kundalini comes from the Hindu religion and refers to a mysterious power that lies dormant in our abdomen but rises up under favorable conditions to awaken and illuminate all the chakras along our spine and allows us to reach our highest potential of enlightenment.

The teaching about kundalini came to Tibet around a thousand years ago and was first publicly taught by the famous saint Milarepa who called this force 'candali'. It is usually called tummo in Tibet (literally 'fierce woman') but teachers like Lama Yeshe use this term interchangeably with kundalini.

Kundalini is known in many spiritual traditions. In parts of Taoism it is called neikung, bone marrow chi or circulating light. In the qabalah tradition it is referred to as the middle pillar exercise and Irina Tweedie describes her kundalini experience within the Sufi tradition in her book 'Chasm of Fire'. Dion Fortune and Gareth Knight made an attempt to compare the different techniques of awakening the kundalini in the yoga tradition, Tibetan Buddhism and the qabalah in their book 'The Circuit of Force'. Catholic Philip St. Romain compares his kundalini awakening to the concept of Holy Spirit in Christianity.

There are many Christian mystics who describe typical kundalini experiences like heat, shaking and experiences of energy without giving a specific name to their cause. For example, the medieval saint Theresa of Avila or Charles Fillmore, the American Christian mystic who co-founded the Unity church, speak of energy experiences that have the hallmark of a kundalini awakening. Theresa of Avila reportedly levitated on numerous occasions, which was witnessed by many people. Supernatural feats like this are only possible with awakened kundalini and there is ample evidence that this amazing power was alive in many Christian saints.

Some Tibetan Buddhists claim that the Tibetan Buddhist tummo awakening is something entirely different from the kundalini awakening in Hindu yoga because the latter focuses on the root chakra while Tibetan Buddhist tummo is supposedly awakened at the navel. This belief is incorrect as in the Tibetan Buddhist system the root and navel are seen as one chakra that can be anywhere between the navel and the perineum. Furthermore, Lama Yeshe makes it clear in his book 'The Bliss of Inner Fire' that Tibetan Buddhist kundalini practices use both the navel as well as the root chakra.

Our Divine Essence

Now we come to the interesting question of what kundalini actually is. In order to understand this mysterious phenomenon we need to go back a little bit and look at our innermost nature. White Tara called this nature our 'divine essence'. This is what she said about it:

> *Your divine essence is your innermost being, your essence. It has two parts: the sea of love and the blissful life force. The sea of love is still, space-like love. The blissful life force is essentially desire and creates all inner and outer experiences and phenomena. Kundalini is particularly concentrated life force.*
>
> *These two parts, love and blissful life force, of your divine essence only ever exist in conjunction and within beings and never on their own or outside of beings. The divine essence in all beings is identical and, in its virgin state, it is felt as rings and undulating spirals of energy meandering through space in endless ecstasy. Pure bliss.*

So, White Tara teaches that the divine essence is our innermost nature and that it is the same in all beings. The question may arise of why we are all so different if, essentially, we all have the same deepest nature. White Tara explains that our differences arise through the very fact that we have lost touch with the bliss of our divine essence and experience our life force in a distorted way. This distorted life force is experienced as our usual confused thoughts and negative emotions. It is this confusion that makes us different and the end of our confusion – our divine essence – is experienced in an identical way in all beings.

The sea of love

What does the sea of love feel like? White Tara explains:

> *The sea of love is absolute love. It is very still, an absolute letting be, giving space and allowing being. It is goodness without distinction. This is why it is called sea of love – it is like the ocean: endless, embracing and all-allowing. The sea of love on its own is not an intentional act of healing – it does not want to change anything. It is sheer benevolent acceptance.*
>
> *In meditation you come nearest to a pure experience of the sea of love in a state of absolute stillness. The breath stops and all movements of the body and mind stop. However, this state is always temporary because the sea of love only ever exists in conjunction with the blissful life force.*
>
> *Most people do not like the sea of love on its own very much because it feels a bit empty and deadening. It needs to be balanced with the blissful life force. The highest state of mind is a state that unites both the life force in its virgin state, which is bliss, as well as the sea of love in perfect balance.*

I found these teachings very exciting and I was astonished to hear that most people do not like the pure experience of the sea of love very much because it is experienced as too empty or even boring. But when I looked at this phenomenon a little bit more closely it became obvious that most of us are trying to *escape* any experience that feels empty, quiet and still. Instead, we are constantly seeking distraction, entertainment and something to 'fill us up with good experiences'.

White Tara said that we need to learn to balance the sea of love with the life force but it is obvious that most of us veer too much in the direction of the life force and rest too little in the stillness of the sea of love. It is for that reason that all world religions admonish us to focus more on love or to become still in meditation.

White Tara went on to explain the function of the sea of love in the bigger picture of the entire universe:

> *Love is the 'glue' of the universe. It can be compared with water that penetrates all living things. As long as water or love is there, it keeps plants and beings alive and in their shape. If you take the water or love out, everything will wither and die. Love keeps the atoms together on the micro-*

level and the galaxies in their beautiful shape on the macro-level.

It is important to remember that White Tara said that the divine essence could only be found within beings and never outside of them as some independent and lifeless material. In her world-view everything is a being, even the entire universe itself.

Recognising the sea of love
White Tara teaches that we cannot recognise the sea of love by ourselves but that we need someone else to show us that love is our innermost nature. White Tara emphasised to me over and over again the importance of the fact that spiritual development can only happen through loving relationships with those who are further on the path than we are.

When I was younger I thought that spiritual development was mainly a question of the right meditation technique but White Tara made it very clear to me that this is not so and that we always need someone else to open our eyes and help us along. We will explore the relational nature of all spiritual development in more depth later on. For now, White Tara tells us this:

> *You cannot recognise the sea of love solely by yourself. You can only be awakened to its existence through the love of others, through other humans or through celestial beings. Once awakened to love, you can awaken others to the awareness of love simply by loving them and uniting with each other in love.*

In order to understand this teaching we can try to imagine how children experience love. It is difficult to imagine that a child who has never experienced love from anybody being able to generate a loving attitude 'out of nowhere'. It is much more likely to imagine a very frightened being, unable to trust anybody and only concerned with his or her own survival. So, White Tara is telling us that we can only be as loving as the most loving being we know.

The life force
The second part of our divine essence is the life force and kundalini is defined as particularly concentrated life force. When we investigate the life force we need to keep in mind that the distinction of the sea of love and the life force is artificial

because in reality those two parts of our innermost nature only ever exist in conjunction. White Tara says:

> *All forms of energy have certain vibrations. By comparison, the sea of love has no vibration, just the potential for it. However, this distinction only exists in theory. In reality the sea of love and the life force always exist in conjunction.*
>
> *All phenomena of the universe are made of the divine essence. The life force is like the building bricks of reality and love is like the cement. There is an endless process of creation going on that can't be stopped.*

So, White Tara is saying is that everything we perceive is made from the life force – inner experiences like thoughts and outer things like plants and matter - but there is also an invisible part of creation that is the sea of love. The sea of love acts like a unifying force that keeps things in the shape that they are. She also points to the fact that everything around us is changing all the time and that new objects and beings are created indefinitely through the ceaseless play of life force, which is essentially our desire.

Recognising the life force
White Tara teaches:

> *Life force is essentially desire or willpower. In its most basic form, life force is simply awareness. Awareness is a form of desire because it is always associated with an intention of what you want to be aware of. In other words, willpower, awareness and life force are essentially the same.*

I initially found it hard to understand how awareness and willpower could be the same because, at first sight, they seem to be quite different faculties of our mind. But White Tara explained that we choose what we focus on and that this choice is inseparable from our awareness. For example, at this present moment we may choose to focus solely on this book and forget most other things that do not interest us, such as the room temperature, our feelings or anything else that may be going on around us.

For most of us these choices about where to direct our focus are largely unconscious. It seems that we are simply aware of what is in our mind or in front of our eyes and ears. But contrary to experience, this is not so. It is common knowledge that a large part of our mind is unconscious and only becomes conscious when we choose to direct our attention towards it. Also, a simple conversation about what has happened in a situation that we experienced with a friend will prove that our experiences differ depending on our choices about where to direct our attention. It is for that reason that White Tara describes awareness and desire as being one and the same thing.

The life force creates what we focus on
Our life force - or our awareness - has an amazing quality – it creates what we choose to focus on. White Tara teaches:

> *Awareness creates what it focuses on. The most basic 'things' you create with your life force are your thoughts, beliefs and emotions. These are the building blocks of your reality because they manifest when you focus on them for long enough.*

> *Therefore, the more awareness, desire or life force you have, the more you can create everything you focus on. So, strictly speaking, everything you focus on becomes part of your being. This is particularly true for everything you focus on for a longer period of time.*

It may appear odd that White Tara teaches that everything we focus on for long enough becomes part of our being. But remember, White Tara explained at the beginning that there are only beings and nothing outside of beings. Her teachings reveal that we created everything in our life – the good and the bad – through our choices of focus. This idea corresponds to the Buddhist understanding of karma. Karma means that our life now is the outcome of our previous actions and that we have the freedom to create a better life by acting in a more loving way.

At first, this idea may seem daunting and I know a lot of people who get upset about the idea of karma because it feels somehow guilt inducing or even like 'blaming the victim'. But we need to understand that most of our karma has been created unconsciously. We often focus on negative ideas simply because we do not know any better or we do it completely unconsciously. For example, nobody gets married with the intention of getting divorced – yet this is exactly what happens to many people because they were not aware of the early warning signs that could have prevented this painful development.

White Tara's teachings are neither about blame nor guilt but about empowerment. What she is saying is that we all have the capacity to create our future exactly in the way we desire by directing our focus on positive altruistic aims.

Using our life force to create the life of our dreams is not an instantaneous process. It requires patience and persistence to see our positive thoughts and desires manifest. Most people find it hard to stay positive in the face of adversity and give in to anger and hopelessness. As a result, they often see their negative thoughts manifesting even though they do not want this on a conscious level.

When White Tara first taught me that we all create everything in our life, I immediately imagined that people would question the fact that we all seem to live within one material universe that we all share like a house. Surely this house (or the universe) was there before us and we have not created it? White Tara refuted this idea by saying:

> *Everybody lives in the universe of his or her own creation. There are universes within universes within universes that all co-exist. People usually share physical matter but all these universes have very different vibrations. That is why some people live in hell while others live in heaven in the same physical environment.*

What the life force feels like

Pure life force in its virgin state is free from any egotistical motives and it feels like bliss. White Tara explains:

> *When you feel the basic life force in its primordial form – undistorted by egotistical fear and greed – you feel it as the five different facets of bliss in the five different chakras. The strongest amount of life force can be felt in the abdomen in the form of kundalini.*

> *Bliss is more dynamic than love. It moves forward and it creates because in bliss there is a subtle intention. This intention is to share the sea of love with others. This is the purest wish.*

Your feelings in your different chakras are always associated with images and thoughts. These images and thoughts are the building blocks of your personal universe. The five different vibrations in the different chakras are the beginning of all phenomena. If they are blissful, you will create a beautiful surrounding and if they are painful and negative, your surrounding will manifest in a painful and negative way, as well.

Unfortunately, most of us are not capable of experiencing the life force as the five facets of bliss in our chakras. Instead, we feel it as our usual negative emotions like anger, greed, sadness and fear. White Tara explains:

It is your intention that determines what happens with your life force. Loving intention produces bliss and fearful intention produces negative emotions, which is a form of distorted life force. As soon as you develop ego-driven fears, the basic life force takes the form of your usual negative emotions. Through your habitual tensing up you lose touch with the bliss of your unspoilt divine essence. Through relaxing and focusing on love and bliss, you can reconnect with your divine essence.

The strength of your desires indicates the strength of your life force and the amount of love and bliss indicates the purity of your life force. If you focus all your desires on love, you have the highest purity and also the highest power.

Let's summarise what White Tara has taught us so far in order to make it clearer: Our deepest nature is the still and all-accepting sea of love in conjunction with the life force. The life force represents our awareness, which contains by nature an element of intention. This intention manifests first in feelings within our chakras with corresponding thoughts and images. If our thoughts and beliefs are loving, they are balanced with the sea of love and can be felt as five different forms of pure bliss in the five chakras. But if our thoughts are selfish, our life force gets distorted into our usual negative emotions like fear, anger and greed. If we focus for long enough on our positive or negative thoughts and images emerging from our chakras, they will manifest in the physical world as positive and negative surroundings. Kundalini is intensified life force located mostly in our abdominal chakra and the more kundalini we have, the more easily we can manifest our desires.

These teachings are extremely powerful. White Tara is actually pointing us to the solution to all our problems and also to the fastest way to reach enlightenment by saying that if we focus *all* of our desires on love, then we will reach highest bliss, love and power in the fastest way possible.

The balance of the sea of love and the life force

White Tara stressed to me over and over again the importance of the perfect balance of the sea of love and the life force. She also explained to me the many negative consequences of the sea of love and the life force within us being out of balance. These are her teachings:

> *The sea of love and the basic life force can never be entirely separated but you often lose the perfect balance of these two qualities of your mind. If that happens, the life force appears as negative emotions and love appears as a passive, depressive or listless state.*
>
> *Most people rest more in the life force pole so that their desires are insufficiently connected to the sea of love. In that case, their desires arise directly out of their distorted life force. They can then be used to manifest mundane wishes, fuel addictions or even be used for evil aims. The remedy for this dynamic is to focus more on love. However, life force can never be entirely separated from love, which is why even the most evil person believes that they are motivated by some benevolent impulse.*

I found this last point exceedingly interesting because it explains why even the most selfish people usually cannot see their errors. Knowing about the dynamic made it easier for me to understand why people can be so selfish, yet see no need to apologise or make amends. But some people also go too far into the sea of love pole. White Tara says about those people:

> *When you go too far into the sea of love so that it gets divorced from life force, it feels like depression. The remedy is to focus on bliss.*

It may be difficult to imagine why focusing too much on love to the detriment of life force can lead to depression. But we need to remember that within the life force lies great power and if we do not have access to this power, we can easily feel victimised and depressed. We can get an understanding of this problem by thinking of a self-sacrificing mother: she is very loving and even self-sacrificing in the way she attends to her husband and children but lacks the sense of power and entitlement to assert her own needs. The natural outcome of this problem is that her family will treat her more and more like the proverbial doormat and this will eventually lead to a feeling of depression.

Finally, there is a third problem that arises when we have trouble going from one pole of our divine essence to the other:

> *Fear arises if you feel stuck in one pole and do not dare to go to the other pole. It happens when you do not dare to relax and trust in the experience of the sea of love or if you are too frightened to go for your desires.*

To summarise: Anger, jealousy and greed arise when we are stuck in the life force pole; depression arises when we are stuck in the sea of love pole and fear arises when we are unable to freely move from one pole to the other.

The perfect union of love and life force is enlightenment

White Tara explains that the perfect union of the sea of love and the life force is called enlightenment or deity-state and that this is the goal of all our spiritual endeavours. She says:

> *The sea of love and the basic life force can never be entirely united or separated; but you should try to bring both these aspects as closely together as possible. Doing this results in a state of greatest happiness and power and ultimately in the deity-state.*

> *The deity-state, or enlightenment, is the perfect balance of the sea of love and life force within you. It is not a state of static frozenness but a dynamic wave of back and forth between the two poles of your divine essence. By uniting the sea of love and the life-energy as closely as possible, all your mental impulses are saturated with love as well as being very blissful and energetic. In that way, the sea of love and the blissful life force come very close to each other without ever entirely merging.*

> *In its purest form this dynamic looks like this: there is at first a union and utter stillness in the sea of love. Then there is a stirring of energy, which is a*

wish to reach out to others to help them to experience the sea of love, as well. This is the beginning of the life force. If your intention remains purely loving, only loving thoughts, feelings and finally a paradise-like surrounding will arise from this first stirring.

I was very amazed and impressed by these wonderful teachings. After digesting them, I asked White Tara how her teaching related to the idea of non-duality that is very popular nowadays. Non-dual teachings assert that there is a final state of mind that transcends all polarities and all subject and object divisions. White Tara gave me this succinct answer:

By focusing all your desires on love, satisfaction is instantly achieved. For that reason one can speak of a non-dual final state. But this state is dynamic – there is always a movement and never a standstill. You always move either towards more love and acceptance or towards more bliss, desire and energy.

These teachings of White Tara were a great surprise to me. I had always thought of enlightenment as a 'state of mind'. White Tara, however, made it clear to me that anything static or one-dimensional is just another form of suffering. The true final 'state', she says, is a form of vibration, a back and forth between the sea of love and the blissful life force in its unspoilt virgin state.

The same misperception can be found in the popular teaching of 'simply being in the here and now' as the be-all and end-all of all our spiritual endeavours. White Tara explains:

Being in the here and now and having long-term goals needs to be united and just like the union of being in the sea of love and the life force it can never be entirely achieved. We need to go back and forth - being in the present moment, which correlates more with the sea of love, and working in a planful way on our long-term goals, which can only be achieved by using the strength within our life force. So, we have always a vibration, a back and forth and never a standstill or a single state.

What is kundalini, after all?

After all these preliminaries it is time to go more deeply into the question what kundalini really is. White Tara explains:

> *When the life force becomes very strong and concentrated in you, it is felt as blissful warmth or heat in your abdomen that enlarges from there to connect all your chakras along the spine in the central channel. This warmth is already one step away from your divine essence. It is the bridge between pure life force energy and physical manifestation.*
>
> *Therefore, one can say that kundalini is the bridge between pure mind and physical manifestation. Every phenomenon begins as the finest stirring of life force in the heart, then goes to the upper chakras where the life force manifests as blissful images and ideas, and then goes to the navel where it becomes stronger and stronger, so that it can finally manifest in the physical world. Another way of putting this is to say that the bliss from your heart and head 'thickens' in the navel.*
>
> *Kundalini contains an element of sexual energy in addition to higher vibrations. It is a mild electromagnetic current and just like an electric cable it gets warm if there is a lot of energy. However, there is more to kundalini than electricity and sexuality. Kundalini also includes the finer spiritual vibrations of the divine essence including the very finest.*

Most people experience their life force most easily and directly in the form of sexual energy. And as we all know, this energy is so powerful that it can create a new human being. Kundalini is our sexual energy and more. It is so powerful that we can actually create our entire personal universe with it. White Tara teaches further:

> *Kundalini can create matter from scratch. It is the same mechanism that makes an egg and a sperm unite and then creates a whole new being. In the same way does the kundalini create your entire life.*
>
> *You usually do not create every single form of matter that surrounds you. Others have done this before you and you are just using these material things. But the amount of kundalini you have determines how much and what kind of matter you can attract into your life.*

So, White Tara is saying that we can create matter from scratch but that we usually do not do that but rather attract matter into our life that has been created by others before us. Therefore, people with awakened kundalini are more capable of consciously creating the life of their dreams compared to people whose kundalini is still asleep.

Why do only certain people have a kundalini awakening?

A question that many people ask is why only some people have a kundalini awakening while others do not? Why does the life force become more concentrated in some people, while most others have to live life without this amazing force? White Tara explains:

> *The kundalini energy comes from everywhere because it is everywhere. It gathers through concentration. It becomes more concentrated because you concentrate. Everybody who concentrates well becomes successful in their field.*
>
> *If you wish to be more loving and happy and you concentrate on that, you will eventually experience a kundalini awakening. The awakening of the kundalini happens when love and power becomes united. If you desire only power or only love the effects will be limited.*

So, White Tara is saying that everybody who concentrates hard, like diligent students for example, become more successful in their field. A kundalini awakening happens through the wish to be equally loving and powerful (or happy) and it is this concentration on these seemingly contradictory qualities that accounts for the intensity of the life force during a kundalini awakening. White Tara explains further:

> *Energy is not a 'thing' that exists in and of itself, but is the result of the friction of two opposing forces. Life force is basically desire. Kundalini energy is the result of the friction of the wish to help others and the disbelief that you can do it. The greater the wish, the greater the initial disbelief and the greater will be the energy that results from it.*
>
> *Once you have overcome this resistance, the appearance of the warmth of the kundalini will stop but your powers will be even stronger. You will become totally trusting and manifest anything by the power of thought by using the kundalini that has been created through your initial disbelief.*

In my work as a kundalini therapist I have observed that these teachings are true. Most clients who come to me have done some form of intensive spiritual or self-development work. That is the wish to be loving and happy that White Tara refers to, which is the union between love and power. Love is the wish for others to be happy and power is the ability to actually be successful with helping others.

When these wishes contrast with low self-esteem or with any idea of being impure, undeserving or somehow 'wrong' then the kundalini creates many uncomfortable symptoms in body and mind. By contrast, if someone has deep trust then the kundalini experience is smoother and more blissful and the person becomes quite adept at manifesting his or her altruistic desires.

Do we really need kundalini?

There are a number of spiritual teachers who assert that one can reach enlightenment without awakened kundalini. White Tara responds to this assertion like this:

> *You can get glimpses of enlightenment without kundalini but you cannot stabilise the experience. If you want to feel the final dynamic state of mind for longer periods of time, you need to have awakened kundalini.*

This view is mirrored by the fact that in Tibetan Buddhism kundalini (tummo) is usually taught in conjunction with Dzog Chen or Mahamudra, which are the practices that teach the direct experience of the true nature of your mind (which White Tara calls the divine essence).

Hindu spiritual teachers also teach that kundalini is necessary to reach enlightenment by piercing the crown chakra and allowing the thousand petal lotus to unfold. Anandamayi Ma was a 20th century spiritual teacher who was considered to be completely enlightened. She clearly states in one of her books that you need awakened kundalini to reach enlightenment.

A kundalini awakening cannot be reversed

Many of my clients who come to me with uncomfortable kundalini symptoms treat it like a disease and hope that I can help them to 'cure' it. But that is impossible and also undesirable as a kundalini awakening is like opening a fast-track towards enlightenment. During the early turmoil of a kundalini awakening this wonderful development may be easily overlooked but it is nevertheless true. White Tara says:

Once the awareness of the kundalini enters your mind, you cannot turn back to the unawareness of the ego-state.

Other researchers of the kundalini phenomenon agree with this observation. Yvonne Kason has written a very well researched book about the kundalini experience called 'Farther Shores'. She states on page 30:

"When an individual is blessed with a kundalini awakening or mystical experience, which is generally accompanied by a kundalini awakening, this heralds the beginning of a life-long process of spiritual transformation of consciousness punctuated with many types of STE [spiritual transformation experiences]. Once the process of spiritual transformation has begun, it generally goes on for the rest of the experiencer's life."

Given that I myself have been in the kundalini process for almost 30 years, I can only agree with this statement. I like to compare this situation to puberty, which cannot be reversed no matter how much we dislike the problems that may come with the awakening of our libido.

The only healthy way to deal with our newly awakened sex drive is to learn to channel it into a loving relationship and the only healthy way to deal with the awakening of our kundalini is to channel it into a life of developing love and wisdom. Both processes entail many challenges but are ultimately very rewarding. While puberty enables us to live a fulfilled family life, kundalini ultimately enables us to reach enlightenment. White Tara says:

Through kundalini you can stabilise the deity-state or enlightenment. Then you feel tireless and full of enthusiasm, are full of benevolent ideas and projects and develop all the supernatural powers.

What kundalini feels like

I will first give White Tara's explanation about what kundalini feels like and will then add a few experiences of my clients and myself. But first White Tara:

Kundalini can be felt anywhere in your body but the navel chakra contains most life force and therefore the kundalini is most easily felt somewhere in your abdomen. You feel the kundalini as a sense of pleasure, heat, pulsating

> *energy, power, motivation, confidence, excitement, fulfilment or a sense of being passionately in love. In fact, falling in love is the strongest kundalini experience one can ordinarily experience.*
>
> *This powerful feeling enlarges up the spine and over your whole body and fills you with intense pleasure and a feeling of inexhaustible energy and power in the experience of the light-body. The colour of the kundalini is a brilliant white or golden.*
>
> *The line of light along your spine widens to the appearance of a white egg and then it spreads out into your surroundings and finally the whole universe is filled with your light and warmth like from a star. When the blissful kundalini goes into your environment it changes your surroundings into the experience of a paradise. Everything pulsates in the same blissful rhythm.*
> *When you have reached the highest state the experience of heat will stop but your powers will be even greater.*

All this sounds rather wonderful but as I have already pointed out kundalini can produce uncomfortable symptoms, as well. White Tara says about this phenomenon:

> *Everything is amplified with kundalini, so there will be a lot more pain if we do negative things. Kundalini makes it impossible to have a defended ego.*

The last paragraph contains a lot of information. White Tara is saying that all our emotions and thought processes are amplified when kundalini is present. This is certainly true for all my clients and myself. Small anxieties can be enlarged to major paranoia under the influence of kundalini and previously repressed anger may suddenly burst forth. This can be very destructive for relationships. But positive feelings are enlarged, as well, and people may find themselves in states of bliss and rapture that were unimaginable before.

White Tara also says that it is impossible to maintain a 'defended ego', when kundalini is present. (The term 'defended ego' is just one example where White Tara uses a sort of language and concept that is not originally Buddhist but suited to my psychological background.)

A defended ego represents our coping mechanisms – the way we defend ourselves from the inevitable frustrations of daily life. We all try to get away from these frustrations but most people's approach to pain avoidance is not very healthy. For example, many people try to ease this pain simply by eating or drinking too much or through a myriad of other addictive forms of behaviour. They literally numb and mask the pain of daily living and the enormous rates of obesity and alcoholism demonstrate just how common this 'approach' is.

There are also psychological defence mechanisms. For instance, people may simply try to ignore their problems or find some superficial explanation to rationalise their needs and hurtful emotions away. They simply 'cope' with living in unfulfilled relationships or oppressive jobs by emotionally shutting down and wearing a 'mask' to the outside world, pretending everything is fine.

White Tara is saying that all these insufficient ways of dealing with pain and frustration do not work anymore when kundalini is present. It seems that we can only live in harmony with awakened kundalini when we 'properly' sort out our issues and start living a life that is healthier and with more integrity compared to how we lived when we still wore our mask. A simpler way of putting this is to say that kundalini makes us more honest. Here is a story of a man I know that demonstrates this point:

> **Case-study: Jonathan, 52 years**
> Before Jonathan's kundalini awakening he was a very calm and gentle man who was happily married and successful in his career as a university lecturer. Secretly, Jonathan prized himself on his 'psychological togetherness' – he rarely got himself worked up about anything and his life ran along quite pleasant and successful pathways. Most people who met Jonathan would describe him as the quintessential English gentleman: emotionally contained, gentle and kind. In other words, Jonathan had a very well defended ego.
>
> Jonathan's kundalini awakened when he met a spiritual teacher who showed him how to focus on the blissful nature of his mind. After some difficulties in the beginning, Jonathan dived deep into the bliss and experienced states of ecstasy that were totally out of reach for him before. In the weeks and months that followed, his body spontaneously contorted into unusual positions that gave expression to many different facets of ecstasy and his heart filled with devotion for his deity so deep that tears started running down his face.
>
> Unfortunately, there was another side to the coin of this wonderful experience and that was that Jonathan suddenly became very opinionated and argumentative. Where before he was accommodating and easy-going, he started

to pick fights about trifling issues with his wife and accused her of being too critical when she protested.

While the bliss in Jonathan's meditation became more and more profound, his marriage started to go to pieces. The 'psychologically together' Jonathan was suddenly seen to throw extremely emotional tantrums; screaming and crying like an out-of-control toddler. What's more, Jonathan became gradually aware of a dark side within himself that he had been totally unaware of. Much to his dismay he recognised petty jealousies, spitefulness, megalomania and sheer selfishness within himself that he never thought he had.

Jonathan was lucky that his spiritual teacher advised him to back off from seeking further states of bliss and instead fully focus on rectifying the character flaws that he had discovered within himself. Doing this was not easy for Jonathan who had, after all, lived to the age of 50 fully convinced that he was a really loving and psychologically healthy person. But with the help of both his teacher and his wife, he learnt to become more aware of his darker motivations and became able to change his selfish impulses into more loving ones.

What constitutes a 'real' kundalini awakening?

Some people writing on the Internet, such as Kurt Keutzer, claim that any experience that does not feel like a freight train going up the spine is not a real kundalini awakening. Keutzer makes much of the difference between ordinary prana (life force) and 'real' kundalini.

According to White Tara this is not a valid distinction. She told me that kundalini is particularly 'concentrated' life force. This means that kundalini is a higher level of life force that can take place by many graduated degrees. At some stage the typical kundalini symptoms will set in and then we are speaking of a kundalini awakening. This can happen gradually or suddenly.

Yvonne Kason has developed a questionnaire to determine whether or not a person has had a kundalini awakening. She says that if a number of kundalini symptoms begin quite suddenly from a specific event onward, you are experiencing a kundalini awakening. This view is in harmony with my own experiences and the teaching of White Tara.

Kundalini awakenings can produce a myriad of different symptoms and it can also occur with many different degrees of strength. The 'freight train'-like experience that Kurt Keutzer describes would catapult most people into a deep crisis. Fortunately, not many people experience this disaster.

Kundalini symptoms

Many books and websites about kundalini focus first and foremost on the physical symptoms of the kundalini. They tend to treat kundalini like an outside energy that has somehow entered a person's body and wreaks havoc. But that is a superficial way of looking at this complex event.

We have learnt from White Tara that kundalini arises from our own divine essence and is therefore foremost an event of the mind. This strong energy merely *highlights* and makes evident our psychological problems and spiritual misconceptions rather than causing them. These problems were there before our kundalini awakening but were largely unconscious. Once kundalini is present, however, the barrier between our conscious and unconscious mind weakens and allows previously unconscious thoughts, motivations and feelings to come to the surface.

If this material is not dealt with properly, people often develop physiological symptoms, very similar to the phenomenon of psychosomatic symptoms. I have been able to corroborate this view through my clinical practice because I consistently see in my clients that the majority of their physical symptoms subside once the underlying negative beliefs and emotions have been rectified.

In chapter five I will go into more detail about kundalini symptoms and in chapter six I will show you how to deal with them. For now, I will summarise the most common and obvious kundalini symptoms that I have observed in my clients and myself. They are:

Experiences of energy churning in one's abdomen or other body parts
Experiences of energy rising up in one's body
Experiences of tingling, jerking, shaking and swaying
Amplified negative emotions alternating with states of great bliss
Increased sensitivity
Experience of one's life being in turmoil
Motivation to improve one's life

Generally speaking, everything is amplified when kundalini rushes through our system. All our unresolved issues are magnified and all our more enlightened aspects are amplified as well - leading to a rollercoaster ride of increased suffering and heightened spirituality and often to feelings of bliss. As one of my clients put it, 'I feel as if the kundalini makes me an amplified version of myself'.

Therefore, uncomfortable kundalini symptoms are not bad. On the contrary, they 'urge' us to resolve our issues and become healthier, more loving and more confident in every way. Even though this process can be difficult and may take a considerable amount of time it serves our deepest purpose, which is to reach our highest potential.

Chapter two
How we Change Through a Kundalini Awakening

In this chapter we will be looking at all the changes that a kundalini awakening evokes in us. These changes will happen on the spiritual, intellectual, emotional and physiological levels and encompass every single area of our life. There is no need to be afraid of all these changes because the main thrust of the kundalini is to awaken a motivation in us to change our life to become more healthy, loving and spiritual in all areas.

Gopi Krishna is one of the foremost writers on the topic of kundalini and he called the kundalini 'an evolutionary force', meaning that it urges us to develop to higher levels of personal and spiritual development. In the words of White Tara:

> *You cannot stay the same with kundalini – it is driving you on to evolve because it makes wrong choices more painful and it also shows you how blissful life could be. If you understand and use this process well, your spiritual quest becomes intensified and you are possessed by the deep wish to reach enlightenment in order to help others.*

Essentially, there is nothing scary or painful as such about a kundalini awakening but our own resistance to changing our life and our lack of understanding can sometimes lead to an initial crisis. But the more we understand what this process is all about and the more willing we are to cooperate instead of fighting it, the easier our process will be.

My own story shows that the kundalini is a benign force. I had an initial crisis that only lasted for roughly a year and the following 29 years were a process of ever growing love, peace and spiritual realisation. The following description of my own kundalini awakening shows quite dramatically how the 'evolutionary force' of kundalini may look in practice. Within one short year my entire worldview, my understanding of myself, my relationship with my friends and family had all completely changed.

My own kundalini awakening

My kundalini awakened at the age of 24 during a series of bio-energetic therapy sessions. This form of therapy uses painful body postures accompanied by screaming to deal with the ensuing pain. It is a rather rough approach that literally breaks through one's ego defences and releases the painful emotions that had previously been suppressed. As a result of this therapy my kundalini awakened, my body shook, quivered and swayed, and my mind underwent a complete transformation.

I was a rather arrogant atheist at the time and struggled with a number of psychological issues that I tried to address with the bio-energetic therapy. But I got a 'deeper cure' than I had bargained for. Within months of my awakening, I experienced such a deep transformation that I turned from a fervent atheist into a devoted spiritual practitioner.

During the bio-energetic therapy, I experienced some very frightening flashbacks to a time when I was a baby, and vividly 'remembered' how I had been abandoned to die in my cot. I have no concrete reason to believe that this was actually true but I know that my mother worked a 50 to 60 hour week at the time and that my siblings and I were brought up by a long succession of nannies. I also know that I had always felt unloved by my mother and that my father wasn't available to me due to his alcoholism. The flashbacks in the therapy felt so real that I cried for hours, desperately wishing to get the parental love that I had never received and despairing at the impossibility of this desire.

Suddenly, my entire existence appeared completely futile and nothing made sense anymore: my political ideas and activism seemed suddenly shallow and short-sighted; the relationships with my friends appeared insufficient to fill that inner yawning hole that had opened up in the depths of my soul, and all my philosophies that I had spun together to help me solve the riddle of life seemed suddenly ridiculous.

Still crippled by the pain of my unhappy childhood, I started to read New Age books that I would not have touched with a barge pole before. I also began dabbling in spiritual concepts that I was not ready for. For example, when thinking about the concept of reincarnation I had a very real sensation of hovering above the ground and not really inhabiting my physical body, which felt extremely disconcerting. I also went to a shamanic workshop, where I was introduced to many strange ideas, which seriously aggravated my confusion.

I was completely unprepared for this sudden turnaround of my mind and felt thoroughly tormented by the breakdown of my previous world-view. What was worse, through the kundalini awakening I also experienced strong rushes of anger that had been unleashed in the hours of pounding pillows and furious screaming that were encouraged in the bio-energetic therapy. Unfortunately, the therapists did not provide any guidance about how to deal with these powerful and destructive emotions and it did not take long before I had fallen out with every friend I had, which added a painful loneliness to my list of problems.

Suddenly I was all alone and the low-boiling depression that I had had for many years virtually exploded into bouts of extreme anguish and despair that brought me to the boundaries of what I could endure. In this terrible crisis, praying to some unknown Goddess seemed to be the only answer and my proud atheistic ego came down with a massive thud.

Just when I thought things could not get worse, they actually got a lot worse. In my confusion and despair I started to pray to 'everything' as I had been taught in the shamanic workshop: to the Goddess, but also to trees and to my grandfather who had passed away a few years earlier. At first, that felt a bit comforting but soon things got out of control because the trees started talking back to me in menacing ways and at night the gentle spirit of my grandfather turned into a frightening monster sitting at my bedside. I was absolutely terrified and seriously thought I was going mad.

Luckily, an acquaintance I confided my troubles in gave me some very good advice. She had some experience with spirits and she simply said, 'you need to retain the ability to say no to these appearances. If you do not like them, just say "no"'. And so I did and to my great relief the frightening experiences with spirits and ghosts ended after a few more weeks of saying 'no' very often.

During these anguished months I started to visit many different spiritual groups in my hometown in order to find a place to live a more conscious spirituality. I did not make this decision in a rational way – I was powerfully drawn to these spiritual places that I had only looked upon with contempt a few months earlier.

About a year after the fateful awakening of my kundalini I set foot in the Tibetan Buddhist centre in my hometown and I just 'knew' I had come home and that I had been 'rescued'. It was as if suddenly the sun was coming into my life; the birds started singing and the state of my mind turned from deepest despair into a sense of overflowing joy that I had never before experienced.

My journals bear witness to this dramatic turnaround and virtually changed overnight from pages full of desperate scrawled ruminations into beautifully designed pages filled with descriptions of my spiritual insights and decorated with pictures of flowers and spiritual symbols.

My happiness about becoming a Buddhist remained and my old crisis did not return. But there were many more lessons to learn, which I will describe in chapter five.

Kundalini turns us towards spirituality

Under the influence of kundalini people become more and more disenchanted with the hunt for material wealth, with superficial appearances and with relationships that are based on shallow values. A strong need for real meaning starts to pervade people's minds and drives them to establish more love and spirituality in every area of their lives. They may dedicate more time to spiritual practice and mystical literature and they will try to adjust every area of their lives to represent deeper and more spiritual values.

The wish to become more loving and compassionate

One of the most beautiful aspects of a kundalini awakening is that it awakens in us the wish to become more loving and compassionate in our private and professional lives. People become more caring about the needs of others and they also care more for the environment.

Beautiful as this wish is, it is not always easy to put it into practice because kundalini also amplifies our negative, selfish and aggressive impulses. This can result in an inner battle, where these positive and negative forces are in conflict with each other. However, if we consciously work through all our inner conflicts, kundalini will help us to become extraordinarily loving and wise.

Paranormal experiences

Many of my clients and as well as myself start to have paranormal experiences after the awakening of the kundalini, which can range from the weird to the wonderful but which can also be outright frightening. I already told you about my own experiences of trees 'talking to me', 'visitations of demons' and feelings of unreality when pondering reincarnation. Here is a selection of paranormal experiences that I have encountered in my clients and myself.

Visions of the divine or angelic beings
Developing special powers like spiritual healing
Seeing faces or UFO's in the dark

Increased experience of meaningful or sinister coincidences
Being abducted by aliens
Having 'real sex' with a person who is not there
Telepathic and clairvoyant experiences with other people or animals
Feeling another being entering into one's body
Poltergeist experiences: unexplained knocking noises in the house or things constantly falling from shelves
Feeling of leaving one's body
Feeling of being taken over by unseen forces
Feeling of being psychically dominated by other people or invisible beings
Feeling of being able to dominate others with the power of thought
Past-life memories
Premonitions in dreams and in waking life

It should be obvious that most of these paranormal experiences can be frightening for someone who does not know what to do about them. I will say more about how to deal with these phenomena in chapter six but for now let me just say that the general Buddhist advice is to not get attached to these experiences – not even to the positive ones. Once we have learnt to deal with these perceptions, they can open the door to a deeper understanding of reality and will awaken abilities within us that we can use to help others in their personal and spiritual development.

Moving away from 'normal society'
Kundalini will awaken desires within us that are out of sync with our normal materialistic society and also from traditional religion. This is in principle a good thing because it allows us to lead a life of deeper meaning and more intense personal spirituality. But if our world-view changes too quickly from the materialistic to the spiritual, some people experience a sensation of alienation from the world. One client put it like this:

Case-study: Chris, 31 years
Chris told me: "One morning I woke up with the thoughts 'what is reality?' and 'what is consciousness?' It completely freaked me out. I thought I was in the movie 'The Matrix' and I could not trust my senses. It was so bad that I got a panic attack and had to wake up my girlfriend. The fear has stayed with me since then."

> Chris got better within the same session when I showed him how to let go of the anxiety with the process of higher consciousness healing. A week later he emailed me and said that he was back to normal. We then had a few more sessions and worked through some issues in his life that were confusing for him.

I myself felt alienation from the world many times. I remember at the age of 30 being on a solo meditation retreat going for a walk. I felt a bit down that day and was wondering why I was going on a walk doing breathing exercises while everybody else my age was busy having families and developing careers. I had a strong sense of not fitting in with 'normal society' and did not understand why I was that way. Obviously, I know it now: kundalini drives us towards the spiritual and that can feel very alienating in a world that is preoccupied with consumerism, competition and appearances on the one hand or with dogmatic religion on the other. White Tara comments:

> *Kundalini may result in great states of bliss in meditation but aloneness and alienation in the ordinary world. The world and other people may appear as very difficult, deficient and even ugly in comparison to your inner state.*

Let me repeat that this sense of aloneness and alienation can be overcome once we understand and embrace the purpose and power of the kundalini more deeply.

Kundalini makes us more sensitive

Under the influence of kundalini, people become much more sensitive in many areas of their lives. This increased sensitivity is directly related to the fact that kundalini is essentially awareness. We simply feel and sense more intensely than before.

The purpose of the heightened sensitivity is to make our mind into a superior instrument that is able to register and process far more information than before. You can compare this situation with the superior awareness of an adult to that of a child. As an adult we can process written information, we can read between the lines, we can pick up on information transmitted in body language and innuendo – all of which a small child cannot do. If a child were suddenly able to access all this information, they would certainly become quite confused. In the same way, we can get confused during the beginning phase of a kundalini awakening until we have learnt to process all the additional information that enters our mind. We may also find sense stimuli like bright light and noise uncomfortable as our senses become more sensitive.

Once we have learnt to handle this over-sensitivity, it will be a great asset. As a therapist, for example, I benefit a great deal from my ability to sense other people's feelings as if they were my own. Also, all our spiritual experiences will become more tangible and 'real' through our heightened sensitivity. We may become increasingly clairvoyant and gain a heightened ability to feel inner bliss. White Tara says:

> *Kundalini increases your awareness. Apart from more positive experience like clairvoyance, this may also bring all sorts of over-sensitivities to sense stimuli like light and particularly noise.*
>
> *Over-sensitivity appears because the numbness of the ego falls away bit by bit. You become like water that can be penetrated by everything instead of being like a numb ice-cube. At the beginning this may hurt and needs time to integrate and subside.*

Here is a list of some of the over-sensitivities that many people experience for periods of time under the influence of kundalini.

Sound: Many people with active kundalini become over-sensitive to levels of noise that most people find perfectly tolerable, like traffic noise, people talking in a restaurant, aeroplanes flying overhead, people using iPods on public transport or people playing music in a neighbouring garden. The noise issue seems to be particular grating with noises that other people make for their entertainment - like drunken people shouting - because these noises are directly opposed to the spiritual thrust of the kundalini. On the other hand, we may experience certain types of music, poems or prayers as so enchanting and wonderful that they induce great states of bliss within us.

Bright lights: For many people exposure to the sun and bright light can become very uncomfortable. This is due to the fact that we already have too much energy on the inside and cannot tolerate more energy like heat and light from the outside on top of that. On the other hand, we may experience the most beautiful inner lights that create great states of bliss within us.

Other people's feelings and thoughts: When kundalini is present we become able to empathise with other people's thoughts and feelings much more strongly. This is greatly beneficial for all our relationships. On the other hand, this can also lead to confusion over whose feelings we are actually feeling – our own emotions or those of the person next to us. It can be confusing to notice a sudden drop in our mood simply through standing next to someone. It can be even more confusing if this person pretends to be happy. It takes time and practice to learn to decipher the onslaught of new signals that we are able to receive. Once we have learnt how to do this, our increased sensitivity will be a great asset in dealing with our relationships more skilfully.

The suffering of others: Our ability to empathise with other people's suffering greatly increases under the influence of kundalini, which is very useful if we work in the healing professions but also a bit disconcerting, initially. I had one meditation student who was in great states of bliss most of the time. She told me that her greatest problem was bursting into tears at the slightest mention of other people's suffering. It was embarrassing for her when this happened in public and she also felt overwhelmed by these experiences. However, it increased her compassion and motivation to help others tremendously.

Increased perception of ugliness and beauty: Under the influence of the kundalini it can become quite difficult to endure disagreeable sights like litter, squalor or even ugly architecture. In our spiritualised and over-sensitive state, these sights can cause us to feel intense sorrow and disgust. On the positive side, our heightened sensitivity can lead to the perception of heart-breaking beauty in ordinary things, people or nature. Even ordinary objects like a chair may appear intensely beautiful.

Increased bodily sensations: All bodily sensations are more pronounced than before. Little itches or pains can become greatly amplified and lead to anxiety and a sense of being ill. We may also become aware of numerous sensations of energy charging through our body, our heart beating or our blood pulsating through our arteries. On the positive side, we may experience blissful sensations running like nectar through our body or sensations that feel like prolonged and most exquisite orgasms in many different parts of our body.

Vibrations in general: Under the influence of kundalini we may enter a house and be overwhelmed by its positive or negative energy, we may have strong good or bad 'feelings' about someone who seems to behave perfectly normally or we may know very clearly who finds us sexually attractive and who does not. It is as if someone switches on a light in a dimly lit room so that we can see a multitude of things that others cannot see. This can be disconcerting and sometimes people are concerned that they are 'spying' on others. On the positive side, our heightened sensitivity will make us into a 'superior instrument' that we can use to do much good for others.

As you can see, this increased sensitivity can be very useful and sometimes also a real nuisance. Unfortunately, there is no easy one-size-fits-all solution to kundalini-related over-sensitivity and I will say more about how to deal with it in chapter six.

Kundalini forces us to deal with our unresolved issues
Not everyone experiences a spiritual crisis as I did when kundalini rises. Many people who have an awakening are already deeply engrossed in a spiritual path and it may simply intensify their religious vigour without bringing on a spiritual crisis.

But quite a few people who are dedicated to a spiritual path have the opposite problem and believe they do not need to deal with their own psychological 'story' because they think that their spiritual practices will take of it. Unfortunately, this is not true.

In the area of psychological growth and relationship skills, everyone has work to do. Sadly, I have met a number of spiritual practitioners who denied this fact and used their practices to actually repress their negative emotions and unresolved psychological issues, instead of working through them. As a result, they often present to the world as an independent persona who is somewhat aloof and unhealthily detached. Not surprisingly, the same people often experience strange psychosomatic pains, chronic fatigue, weird anxieties and depression, with or without active kundalini.

I have found in my clinical practice that many of these symptoms result from the repression of unresolved psychological issues in the way in which we relate to others and how we deal with our emotions. Once kundalini is present, all psychological and psychosomatic symptoms are greatly amplified and it becomes increasingly difficult to maintain the 'spiritually advanced' persona. It is through this amplification of our emotions that the kundalini 'forces' us to find more genuine solutions to our problems. The good news is that once we attend to our personal issues, these symptoms start to subside.

Yvonne Kason echoes my experience in her book Farther Shores on page 284, where she writes: *"We all have unresolved psychological issues and unhealthy belief patterns. Everyone involved in the process of spiritual transformation eventually discovers this. After many years of working in this field it seems increasingly clear to me that what I call psycho-spiritual housecleaning is an absolute essential – and unavoidable – part of the process of spiritual transformation."*

And White Tara puts it like this:

> *People think that they become tougher and tougher on the spiritual path but that is not true. All good spiritual practice makes you happier on the one hand but exposes your weaknesses simultaneously. This is because spiritual practice takes your ego-defences away. Through this process kundalini unleashes the entire content of your unconscious mind with all its problems and unpleasantness.*

What follows is a list of typical issues that may come to the fore during the kundalini process and which cannot be ignored. I myself have experienced every single one of them. There is no one-size-fits-all solution to these issues. They simply need to be resolved in a thorough way, either alone or with the help of a therapist. In chapter six I will go into more detail about how to get over kundalini-related problems.

Amplified emotions

All our emotions are strongly amplified once kundalini is awakened. White Tara told me:

> *With fewer ego-defences your negative emotions will appear much more painful than when you were quite numb.*

Small anxieties may develop into major anxieties; mild irritations may suddenly explode into temper tantrums and feeling a little down may transform into anguish and despair. But positive emotions are enlarged as well and can lead to wonderful states of bliss and ecstasy.

Typically, people with active kundalini find themselves on a rollercoaster of intense emotions that regularly peak and trough. The good news is that our amplified emotions 'force' us to develop psychologically at an accelerated rate and once we have worked through our neurotic problems, we will emerge wiser and more compassionate than the average human being.

Resurgence of old emotional wounds and traumas

Most of my kundalini clients experience the resurgence of old psychological topics, wounds and traumas. Some of these problems may have been completely unconscious but now demand urgent attention.

Some clients who have already done a lot of work on themselves find this frustrating, imagining they had dealt with these issues long ago. But under the amplifying influence of the kundalini, any remnants of these old problems are thrust to the surface and need to be worked through more thoroughly than before. Even though this can be disconcerting in the beginning, it is also a wonderful opportunity for personal and spiritual growth that will help us tremendously to advance on our spiritual path.

Sexual issues

I have noticed that a rather high percentage of my kundalini clients have sexual issues. Typically, these clients have to deal with their repressed sexuality. While many people go through life in a sexually repressed way, this is no longer possible under the influence of the kundalini. The frustration and inner conflicts become so strong that they can no longer be ignored and demand a more thorough solution. On the positive side, kundalini can help people to have a more satisfying sexuality and intensified orgasms.

Some people with awakened kundalini experience sexual over-arousal, which can be confusing as well as uncomfortable and frustrating. In yet other clients, the sexual drive stops altogether, which can bring difficulties in a partnership and a worrying feeling that there is 'something wrong' with them, given that in our modern society a high sex drive is equated with emotional health. However, for some people the bliss that is generated by the kundalini makes sexual pleasure look crude and inferior in comparison.

When kundalini awakens, our sexual orientation may change in astounding ways. People who were heterosexual all their lives may suddenly notices gay or lesbian urges or vice versa. This can be quite disorientating or even frightening but is an essentially harmless experience. Nobody is forced to act on these impulses and they can be viewed simply as a broadening of our sexual self.

If someone has experienced sexual abuse, they are bound to remember it once kundalini is active and feel a strong urge to come to terms with this upsetting trauma. There are also clients who experience memories of sexual abuse that seem strangely unreal and disconnected from what they actually experienced in their life. In my work as a transpersonal therapist I have explored these kinds of memories in detail with my clients and we often come to the mutual conclusion that they probably come from a past life. Once this insight has been reached, the stress around this topic subsides very quickly.

Overall, working through our sexual issues and broadening our sexual self is a process that will be very rewarding and help us to be profoundly at peace with ourselves.

Guilt feelings

Many of my clients experience sudden realisations of how hurtfully they have behaved to others and develop guilt feelings as a result. Before the kundalini awakening, they may have dealt with their guilt by ignoring it or by denying it. But once kundalini is active these defence mechanisms no longer work and it is important to take these guilt feelings seriously and try everything we can to make amends. The positive result will be that we will feel unburdened and more at peace with others and ourselves.

> **Case-study: Barbara, 54 years**
> Barbara had already had ten sessions with me when she suddenly remembered how she had punished one of her daughters by shutting her out of the house at night. The memory made her feel distraught and extremely guilty. It had been a one-off event and nothing similar had happened before or after. Barbara had always thought of herself as a good parent but when she was in her kundalini process it suddenly became clear to her how much she had traumatised her daughter. In order to put the matter right, she visited her daughter and humbly asked for forgiveness and it improved their relationship a great deal.

Issues with repressed anger

Most of my kundalini clients have issues with repressed anger. This dynamic often happens to people who try to become more spiritual, loving, tolerant and patient. Even though this is a very positive intention, it often results in the anger getting repressed instead of being accepted and worked through.

This inner conflict is aggravated through the energy of the kundalini, which makes all our inner dynamics more intense. In my experience, many painful physical symptoms are due to the dynamic of repressed anger. The good news is that as soon as the anger is recognised and dealt with, the physical symptoms subside in a matter of hours or days. Here is a typical example:

> **Case-study: Claudia, 64 years**
> Claudia had been participating in bio-energetic therapy for many years and had experienced a kundalini awakening as a result. During the sessions we had together we worked through many of her issues and her intense anxiety very much subsided. But she still suffered from pain and a sense of irritating tingling in her lower back.
>
> Claudia assumed that these problems were coming from an experience of sexual abuse she had experienced as a child and we worked through this trauma until the emotional charge had completely subsided.
>
> Claudia experienced a great sense of healing but, unfortunately, her back pain persisted and continued to cause her a great deal of suffering. I asked Claudia to gently massage the area of pain and tingling and it was not long before she experienced strong feelings of anger without knowing what the anger was about. I asked Claudia to think about all her close relationships and to check whether anybody was making her angry.
>
> To Claudia's surprise, she discovered how angry she was with her sister, with whom she had a very close relationship. As we were talking about her feelings towards her sister the pain and tingling in her back completely disappeared, which was highly unusual.
>
> I then showed Claudia how to resolve the relationship with her sister by sending love to her. Claudia practiced this and also had a conversation with her sister to clear the air. Much to her surprise and relief, her back problems disappeared. However, after a few months the pain returned and this time we discovered that she was repressing anger towards her husband. I helped Claudia to communicate more honestly with her husband and to let go of old grievances through sending love to him. Again, the back pain almost immediately subsided and stayed away.

Unhealthy patterns in relationships

Under the influence of kundalini our relationships cannot continue in the way they have before and we are called to bring them to a higher and healthier level. White Tara says:

> *You become able to see many negative things in yourself and others that you didn't see before, due to the fact that kundalini equals awareness. For example, you may start to see the many forms of selfishness, stupidity and envy in yourself and others. This can be quite shocking and saddening.*

There are many unhealthy patterns in relationships but the two main negative patterns are selfishness (typically men) and submissiveness (typically women). Once kundalini is active, these unhealthy relationship patterns cannot continue because the kundalini intensifies the pain arising from these dynamics.

It is clear that making major changes in relationships can create some upsets and, in some cases, it may even cause break-ups. However, the end result of this development will be a more loving relationship with someone who shares your values and your wish to grow spiritually.

Case-study: Chris 33 years

Chris' kundalini had awakened two years before and he contacted me because he had developed strange anxieties and upsetting dreams. I asked Chris how the rest of his life was going and he said that everything was going very well; that his work was fine and that he was very much in love with his girlfriend and had recently proposed to her. On closer investigation it turned out that the onset of his strange anxieties had coincided with his proposal to his girlfriend.

At first Chris denied that anything was wrong in his relationship but eventually he admitted that his fiancée had a bad habit of getting really drunk every few months. He had tolerated this behaviour for many years and did not even see much wrong with it because in their social circle many people drank a lot. However, Chris himself never got involved with alcohol or drugs and was deeply engaged in spiritual practices.

Chris and I concluded that the strange anxieties and upsetting dreams were actually telling him symbolically just how worried he was about marrying someone with an uncontrollable drinking habit. Chris agreed that he had to make changes in his relationship and that he could not go through with the

> marriage as things stood. As a result of these insights, his anxieties subsided considerably.

In addition to the changes in our closest relationships, virtually everyone in the kundalini process finds it impossible to carry on relating to their parents and relatives in the way they have done before. All unhealthy family patterns will suddenly become intolerable and 'force' the person to make sometimes dramatic changes. It should be obvious that this process takes time and cannot be completed overnight. But the positive result will be that you will become free from debilitating and oppressive family dynamics so that you can realise your true potential.

Psychosomatic pains, fatigue, 'weird' physical symptoms and 'old' diseases

People who are going through a kundalini process often experience a plethora of physical symptoms, which can range from the weird to the painful. Sometimes these symptoms relate to an old illness while at other times they are completely new. In all cases, it is important to clarify with a qualified physician whether you are dealing with real illnesses before seeing them as kundalini symptoms.

Many of my clients have the impression that kundalini is some sort of foreign force that moves around in their body and 'gets stuck' or 'blocked'. But we need to understand that this is a simplistic view and that kundalini is not an outside force that is tormenting us. The kundalini and we ourselves are one and we are simply experiencing our own inner conflicts in an amplified form. White Tara says:

> *All physical and psychological problems resulting from kundalini awakening are the result of your contradictory intentions. There is no kundalini energy that moves around on its own accord and creates problems. There is only the friction between your more loving and more selfish desires, which fight with each other.*

In my observation, physical kundalini symptoms subside once we learn to penetrate our emotional and psychological issues with pure love. By contrast, any attempt to get rid of physical symptoms through some sort of energy healing usually back-fires because we are trying to get rid of the symptom without really dealing with the problem. I will say more about how to deal with kundalini symptoms in chapter six. For now, I would like to simply make the point that physical symptoms of kundalini are often pointing us to unresolved emotional problems, spiritual misperceptions or relationship issues. Once these issues are resolved, we will find ourselves in a much better state – physically *and* psychologically. The following example demonstrates this point:

> **Case-study: Michael, 45 years**
> Michael had awakened kundalini and went to an acupuncturist because he suffered from debilitating fatigue. The day after his first acupuncture session he suddenly became completely impotent. The acupuncturist vigorously denied that this was caused by the acupuncture and maintained that acupuncture was completely free of side effects. It took my client roughly 6 weeks before his potency came back but he was badly shaken by this occurrence.
>
> When he addressed his fatigue in our sessions we discovered that it was his way to repress anger. Once he understood this dynamic and addressed his annoyances more openly, his fatigue went away.

Selfishness and pride

Many people who follow a spiritual path think of themselves as being loving, good and honest when in fact they do not possess these qualities to the extent they believe. It is typically men who suffer from these prideful delusions.

When kundalini is present the prideful person will sometimes attract a person, for example a spiritual teacher or a partner, who confronts them with their selfishness until it can no longer be ignored. The prideful person confronted in this way will feel a mixture of anger and gratitude – anger for having their cherished ego attacked, and gratitude because they realise that they need this criticism in order to mend their selfish ways.

In a worse scenario the selfishness and pride will get amplified through a kundalini awakening due to the general amplification of all our mental and emotional patterns. It is this dynamic that accounts for all spiritual teachers who started out in a well-intentioned way but were corrupted by their fame and the devotion of their disciples. It is this unmitigated self-aggrandisement that is the greatest danger of a kundalini awakening.

Luckily, most problems that come to light during a kundalini awakening will have a strongly humbling effect on us, mitigating the danger of self-aggrandisement. It does not serve a 'big ego' to experience sudden and severe psychological problems, particularly if we considered ourselves 'sorted out' or even 'spiritually advanced'.

Just remember Jonathan in the first case study – it was an extremely humbling experience for him to find himself having temper tantrums.

Nobody likes humbling experiences, but we should be grateful if they happen to us because humility is the antidote to an inflated ego and an inflated ego is the greatest obstacle to our spiritual growth. Therefore, the humbling influence of kundalini will greatly advance us on our spiritual path in the fastest way possible.

Kundalini forces us to improve every area of our lives

So far we have discussed how kundalini 'forces' us to develop spiritually and psychologically. But that is not all. We are also 'asked' to improve all outer areas of our life – our work, relationships, diet, home and everything else that is not in alignment with our highest spiritual aim. In the words of White Tara:

> *The heightened awareness of kundalini makes it impossible to put up with any unhealthy relationship or situation that you have submitted to before and 'forces' you to seek an environment that is more conducive to spirituality. This can be a very difficult adjustment process.*

In the following paragraphs we will discuss a number of areas that may have to be improved once our kundalini awakens.

Changes in our professional life

Many people feel drawn to change their work-life under the influence of kundalini in order to find something that allows them to be of more service to others. For example, one of my kundalini clients was an accountant and another was a policeman. Neither of them saw much meaning in their professions any more. The policeman said that he could no longer stand the rough and racist remarks of his colleagues and the accountant said that he did not see any more meaning in simply trying to earn as much money as possible. Both wanted to move into helping professions like massage therapy or teaching yoga. This 'spiritualisation' of our work-life is typical under the influence of kundalini.

Problems may arise if we are not in a position to change our job or profession due to financial responsibilities or other circumstances. And even if we change our job to become a healer or therapist, we might find ourselves incapable of attracting sufficient clients to make a living. Yet other problems arise when people feel they have a vocation in life but cannot identify this special mission. This too can be a frustrating and painful experience.

However, if we fully embrace our inner drive to seek a more rewarding work experience, we will be able to achieve this in most cases through determination and persistence.

Changes in our relationships

As mentioned before, our relationships, too, often need a major overhaul once kundalini has been awakened. Marriages often need dramatic improvement if they are not to end in divorce. Friendships that do not serve our spiritual development are often abandoned and even our relationships to members of our original family often need to change dramatically and in many cases become a lot more distant. Making all the changes can be difficult but will be very rewarding in the long run, once we have surrounded ourselves with people who match our values and spirituality.

> **Case study: Mark, 45 years**
> Mark was deeply interested in meditation from his teenage years onwards and experienced his first kundalini awakening at the tender age of 19 after spending a week in a Buddhist monastery in Nepal. As a result he embarked on an even more intense spiritual quest and spent many winters with his Hindu Guru Amma in India.
>
> In the interview that I conducted with Mark he told me that he found his kundalini awakening overall very positive. However, he admitted that the split-up from his partner and mother of their two children was due to his intense interest in spiritual development that his wife did not share. He now lives alone and felt that was the right thing for him.

In some people a kundalini awakening evokes the wish to abandon family and friends and live as a hermit in a spiritual retreat. Gopi Krishna, for example, talks about this desire in his autobiography 'Living with Kundalini', although he never actually did it.

In my own marriage, I also experienced conflicts with my husband due to my own accelerated pace of development. It took patience and determination on both our parts to work through these issues but it enriched our relationship profoundly.

Changes in our living accommodation

As the kundalini process goes on, many people experience a greater and greater need to live in a quiet countryside setting. Mystics and spiritual seekers have withdrawn into hermitages throughout history and across spiritual traditions. I have no doubt that this happened due to their awakened kundalini, which 'demanded' that they made this sacrifice, despite the dangers and discomfort that this may have entailed.

It is no different for modern-day spiritual seekers who may find that city life becomes intolerable under the influence of kundalini. Obviously, it can be difficult to find a perfect country retreat, which for most people is a real luxury. However, I think that if someone makes this need a priority, they will eventually be able to find a place that suits their spiritual need for tranquillity.

My own biggest challenge over the last ten years was the conflict between harmonising my need for a quiet living in nature with the need to work as a therapist. In order to reach enough clients I really should live in an urban surrounding but my heightened sensitivity would have made it impossible to put up with the noise and vibrations of living in such close proximity to so many people. Reluctantly, we moved to a small village and I only saw a few clients a week. But I was quite unhappy about this because I really love my work. Moving to a city was definitely out of the question given the raw nature of my nervous system. Eventually, I was able to build an online therapy practice and we were able to move even more deeply into the country.

Changes in diet and health care

Once the kundalini is flowing, many people feel drawn to become vegetarians and change their diet to become much healthier. Junk foods like fizzy drinks, cheap fats and overly processed foods suddenly appear disgusting and people actively seek to find ways to eat more fresh and wholesome food. The advantages of doing this should be obvious and as people feel better physically it will also help them to feel better emotionally.

Some people with awakened kundalini feel an intense wish to go on prolonged fasts. I myself fasted for around three whole months on and off within the time span of two years. This was of course a bit extreme and I do not encourage people to copy me. Gopi Krishna describes in his autobiography how he repeatedly stopped eating altogether when his kundalini was flowing strongly and how doing this seriously endangered his health.

People also change their attitude towards their body and health to become more wholesome and natural. The general heightened sensitivity of the kundalini process is responsible for the fact that people often become averse to ordinary prescription drugs. Unfortunately, any form of energy healing such as reiki, acupuncture or homeopathy can produce severe side effects, as well, if kundalini is active. I myself experienced these peculiar dynamics several times. For example, I could not wear any jewellery with crystals for many years because it produced severe pain. When I tried magnetic therapy I noticed that I became unusually anxious and when I used a homeopathic remedy I felt a very uncomfortable sense of suffocation for six weeks. I will say more about these problems and what to do about them in chapter six. The following case-study describes how Harry changed virtually every area of his life after a sudden kundalini experience.

> **Case study: Harry, 28 years**
> Harry was a bright young man but had left school without any qualifications and had been a drug addict for several years. He contacted me after experiencing a classical kundalini experience after taking drugs at a music festival.
>
> Once kundalini was active, Harry became very ecstatic for a short while but then developed severe anxiety about going mad. He sometimes saw frightening demons and had the most terrifying dreams.
>
> I showed Harry how to calm his anxiety with the anti-anxiety technique and how to send love to the terrifying creatures he perceived around him. Within a matter of two months, Harry felt much better and started to make dramatic changes to improve his life in every respect. He stopped seeing his old drug-related friends, he explored a career change, and he started to eat a vegetarian diet and practiced yoga every day.
>
> However, there was one massive problem that was not easy to improve and that was his relationship with his girlfriend Sarah. Sarah was convinced that Harry must have been suffering from some sort of obsessive compulsive disorder to be suddenly spending so much time and effort on things like yoga and healthy cooking. Sarah was beside herself with distress because she could not even recognise her old boyfriend with whom she had spent many years taking drugs, getting drunk and watching horror movies. Harry did not want to do any of these things anymore, which made Sarah angry and upset.
>
> I tried very hard to explain to Sarah that Harry's development was essentially healthy even though it looked excessive and incomprehensible to her.

> Unfortunately, I was not successful and after fighting for a few months, Harry and Sarah split up.
>
> Harry was a bit sad about this development but relieved at the same time because it was clear to him that he had changed so much that he had no future with his Sarah.

Finally, the really positive changes

Throughout the preceding pages I have touched on the many positive changes that result from the kundalini process but this optimistic message may have become a bit lost among my descriptions of the many difficulties that may accompany even the most benign kundalini process.

Despite all these possible difficulties, a kundalini awakening is the most wonderful thing that can happen to a spiritual seeker. According to Tibetan Buddhist teaching, we can only reach enlightenment on the basis of awakened kundalini. The Tibetan equivalent of kundalini practice – tummo - is said to be the foundation of all the advanced practices. Simply put, without the energy of active kundalini we do not have the necessary power to sustain higher states of mind for long. What follows are all the wonderful experiences that await you if you are prepared to deal whole-heartedly with the more challenging aspects of a kundalini awakening.

Bliss

Among the most tangible and most easily obtained benefits of awakened kundalini are states of bliss, ecstasy and rapture. The easiest way to imagine the bliss of awakened kundalini is to think of the ecstatic sensation of an orgasm. Imagine that this most pleasurable feeling spreads out and penetrates every part of your body and mind – that is bliss. My teacher Garchen Rinpoche used to say, 'the bliss will become so strong that someone could stick 600 needles into you and you would not notice it'.

There are different facets or nuances of bliss in the different chakras in our body. It is difficult to describe these different qualities of bliss because they are so unusual that our language does not have many apt words for them. However, I will try to describe them and please bear with me if these descriptions do not mean that much to you. As your own kundalini process deepens, you may come up with your own and possibly better descriptions:

The bliss in our head feels like heavenly pleasure – just like being in paradise or heaven.
The bliss in our throat feels more joyful – as if you have the most amusing banter with someone you love.
The bliss of the heart feels like deepest love – like the moment of the deepest care that you ever felt with a pet, your children or your partner.
The bliss of the solar plexus fills us with a sensation of deepest peace – like sitting next to a still lake in perfect tranquillity.
The bliss at the navel feels like the overflowing joy you would feel if all your dreams were suddenly fulfilled.

The hallmark of all these different forms of bliss is that they feel complete. There is no such thing as half an orgasm, similarly the bliss of kundalini feels total and complete. White Tara says:

> *The bliss of kundalini is something out of the ordinary. It is exactly this extraordinary quality of the bliss that makes it so special. You feel removed from the mixed experience of earth and you are plunged into an exalted state that you would call paradise. It is different from any earthly joy.*

Creativity

Through the rise of kundalini our creative forces are strongly stimulated. I once read about a man who was struck by lightning and survived (a rather forceful kundalini awakening). In the weeks that followed this incident, he noticed some strange changes in himself. The most remarkable change was that he started to hear the most beautiful symphonies in his mind. They were so beautiful that he felt compelled to write them down. But this man had no previous knowledge or interest in music and he actually had to learn how to write music before he was able to transcribe what he perceived through his inner ear. Once he had gained a basic knowledge of music he recorded very complex and long pieces of music.

I myself have noticed the creative force of kundalini many times and I believe that the development of my psychotherapeutic method, higher-consciousness healing, is a direct result of my kundalini awakening. Higher-consciousness healing is a new form of psychotherapy and it is so effective that it can heal depression, anxiety and relationship problems within weeks. I have written proof of this rather exaggerated sounding claim from hundreds of my clients.

I also went through a phase where I felt inspired to create beautiful Buddha images (*tankhas*), which I embroidered for hundreds and thousands of hours.

During another phase, I started to write poems to give expression to the beautiful energy that I felt within me. But due to my main interest of helping others, my creative juices always flowed mostly into writing books and trying to find ways to help my clients more effectively.

In some cases, our creativity may appear as a sudden gift, enabling us to become a successful artist very quickly. But in most cases, the development will take a lot of hard work and it may take many years until we can speak of some level of success. The gift of kundalini is to make this work more successful compared to the average person.

Better health, longevity and beauty

The power of the kundalini can also be used for spiritual healing and enhanced resistance to disease. As with all the other special powers that arise with a kundalini awakening, these gifts do not come fully formed. Usually, it is necessary to develop the gift for healing through many hours of dedicated practice of a system like reiki or faith healing. You may even be able to create your own healing modality, as I did, but I would assume that it will take many hours of work until it is fully developed.

Kundalini also makes people more beautiful and sexually attractive. Furthermore, you will have more energy and a more youthful appearance than other people of your age. This is due to the fact that kundalini constitutes the life force, the very force that gives us life and is so much more plentiful in younger people. All this is of course a rather nice by-product of this awesome power but obviously we should not strive for a kundalini awakening for these more worldly reasons alone.

Deeper insight, intuition and intelligence

As we have already learnt, kundalini is essentially awareness and due to this awareness our mental faculties, like logical thinking, reasoning, the ability to make moral judgements, foresight, intuition and psychic ability will all improve as well. We may also become able to see connections and patterns in our field of interest that noone has seen before, possibly enabling us to make amazing discoveries.

You will also become more adept in exploring your unconscious mind. Instead of fearfully shrinking away from your own inner darkness, you will be able to go on a deep 'inner journey' and come back with an understanding about human nature that may be highly inspiring for others.

Kundalini will also enable you to better understand religious scriptures that may have appeared incomprehensible to you before. You may even become able to read spiritual books by enlightened masters and fully empathise with what they are saying.

Finally, kundalini will enable you to develop the highest wisdom about the deeper nature of the universe, God and the human mind. Only kundalini allows us to penetrate deeply into these mysteries that have puzzled humankind from beginningless time.

Liberation from our ego

In the experience of rapture and bliss something remarkable happens: our usual sense of self fades and is replaced with a sense of openness, freedom and joy that is experienced as a great sense of liberation.

There is no feeling anymore of having a personal core or of having a limited sense of self that starts and ends where our body starts and ends. Instead, we experience ourselves as an endless, glittering space brimming with the most joyful, loving and exhilarating potential.

This experience is the most enthralling state of mind that one can possibly imagine. It is so free, so loving and so satisfying that it cannot be compared to any other pleasure that we might experience through our senses. In the Buddhist literature, this experience is referred to as emptiness or 'non-self'. This is not yet enlightenment but rather an important preliminary step towards it.

Before we experience the state of non-self, we do not realise just how much we are weighed down by having to protect our personal sense of ego and how much suffering we experience through being 'shackled' to our personal history. Only when these constrictions fall away and we taste the freedom of emptiness do we understand why it is said in Tibetan Buddhism that 'the attachment to the ego is the source of all suffering'.

I should make it clear at this point that the experience of non-self is not something that arrives suddenly and then stays stable throughout the remainder of our life. All the positive changes described in this chapter are gradual; they come and go and they slowly change the sense of who and what we think we are. I personally would be very suspicious of any spiritual teacher who claims to have had a few experiences of non-self and then gives the impression that they remained in that state from that point on.

The humble and honest truth is that we will be ricocheting between our old sense of self and our new sense of liberation for a very long time and that the stabilisation of our new state of mind will only happen slowly and will probably never be entirely complete within this life-time.

I can also attest to the fact that under stress our old sense of ego, with all its pain-inflicting 'stories', can and will come back with a vengeance. Our development can be gauged by the time it takes to return to our new sense of 'non-self'. Here is a list of signs that we are coming nearer to the state of non-self.

Freedom from our personal past: Everybody identifies with their personal history, their childhood upbringing and the positive and negative experiences that have shaped their character. When we evolve through kundalini, all our past experiences can still be remembered but they do not feel like 'me' or 'mine' anymore and they do not carry any special emotional charge beyond the fact that they may have been generally sad or happy. For people who were weighed down by a traumatic or disadvantaged childhood, this is an unbelievably wonderful liberation.

Freedom from the need to protect our ego: The average person feels a great need to protect their personal ego from the threat of being criticised or ridiculed. People usually have an arsenal of ego-defences that allow them to see everything that goes wrong as other people's fault, while maintaining a positive and faultless idea of themselves. But doing this comes at a heavy cost as these strategies can make us very anxious, depressed and angry. Once the kundalini process has enabled us to let go of this limiting way of life, we will be able to take criticism more impersonally, using what is useful and disregarding the rest without getting upset in the process. All social inhibitions and anxieties fall away and we are able to laugh at our faults and have unshakeable confidence in the core of our inner goodness.

Freedom from restrictions imposed by our cultural and religious background or by gender, class, race and sexual orientation: Everybody feels either disadvantaged or privileged due to their cultural and religious background or due to their gender, social class, race and sexual orientation. These are deep-seated prejudices that we all suffer from, which can never be fully overcome unless kundalini sets us free. But once kundalini is present, it allows us to overcome these limitations. As an example, I would like to cite Saint Catherine of Siena who was the daughter of a humble cloth dyer in medieval Italy. After experiencing an intense spiritual transformation, she went on to be highly influential in the politics of her times – a feat that should have been impossible given her gender and social class.

Freedom to be whatever and whoever you want to be: Once we are free of our personal past and the limitations of our culture and society, we can go on to be whatever and whoever we want to be. We can achieve great feats and eventually identify with a deity, assume a divine body and reach full enlightenment.

Power and supernatural power

With kundalini comes power. Diving deep into our unconscious mind can be difficult at first but if we do not resist this process, it can also unleash a lot of personal power. Simply speaking, we have a lot more energy at our disposal that is normally lost in numerous ego defences designed to repress our negative emotions and unacceptable desires. Once we have learnt not to fear our deeper impulses we can use this surplus energy for any goal or project we desire.

There are many spiritual teachings that advocate the use of the power of our mind to manifest our dreams. I myself have outlined this process in my book 'Advanced Manifesting – Tibetan Buddhist teachings to manifest your dreams'. You may have had stab at manifesting yourself and wondered why it seems to work sometimes better and sometimes worse. The answer to this question lies, of course, in the amount of kundalini that flows into your desire. The more kundalini you have at your disposal, the more successful you will be at manifesting your heart's desire. White Tara says:

> *The more heat there is in your experience of kundalini, the more power you have. All your thoughts and emotions become extremely powerful and you can command your reality through visualising and enveloping people with bubbles of love and kundalini. Finally, you can simply command reality with the power of thought.*

I think it is obvious that what White Tara describes here is a very advanced state that can only take place once we have developed supernatural powers or *siddhis*. The key to developing these powers lies within the concentration on certain chakras, filling them with the power of kundalini and passionately wishing for the *siddhi* to occur for the best of all beings. This needs to be practised with complete concentration over an extended period of time and of course with the purest motivation to benefit *everybody,* as impure desires can otherwise lead to masses of bad karma for life-times to come. Here is a list of supernatural powers that can be activated through the development of kundalini:

Clairvoyance (knowing what other people are thinking and feeling)
Clairsentience (feeling other people's feelings)
Channelling the words of a higher being
Communicating with spirits
Influencing other people with the power of thought
Spiritual healing
Accurately foretelling the future
Power to seduce and fascinate others (charisma)
Bi-location (being at two place at the same time)
Telekinesis (moving objects with the power of mind)
Ability to run very fast (this was very useful in Tibet before cars and aeroplanes were introduced)
Levitation (lifting one's body into the air)
Influencing the weather
Materialisation of objects
Waking the dead

Naturally, our *siddhis* will first materialise in the area of our most passionate interest. For someone in the medical profession, for instance, this desire may be geared towards healing and so this person may develop the supernatural power of spiritual healing. My own deepest desire was to get answers to the many metaphysical questions I had, which is why I developed the ability to channel White Tara's words. It took me several years to develop this gift and to really trust that I had this ability. The same can be said about all supernatural powers. It often takes years of concentrated work in order for these gifts to blossom.

Wim Hof is a Dutchman who learnt the tummo exercise, which is the Tibetan Buddhist practice for awakening of kundalini. He used it for the rather frivolous purpose of becoming resistant to cold and created many media stunts like running a marathon barefoot in the snow, which would be highly dangerous for ordinary mortals. In his book 'Becoming the Iceman' Wim describes how it took him many years of dedicated training before his ability to resist the cold became somewhat 'supernatural'.

Many people dabble in supernatural powers like fortune telling or using the pendulum, with very unreliable results. This is because they lack the amount of kundalini that makes these feats possible in the first place. Other people seem to be born with the gift of sight and other special abilities. From a Buddhist perspective, this happens because these people developed a certain amount of kundalini during past lives, which they can tap into in the present.

It is important to understand that the possession of supernatural powers, developed in a past life or in this one, is not a sign of spiritual advancement. These gifts can actually be used for frivolous or even evil aims. My teacher, Garchen Rinpoche, always emphasises that spiritual realisation is measured by one sign alone, and that is how much love we have for others.

Both Hindu and Buddhist teachers warn us not to get attached to our budding supernatural powers and to use our kundalini for enlightenment, instead. Enlightenment means clearing out our mind of every trace of egotism and dedicating ourselves fully and completely to loving and helping others. For that reason, supernatural powers do not need to be rejected but, instead, should be used solely for loving purposes.

Unfortunately, many well-known kundalini teachers were unable to heed this all-important advice and used their amazing powers to seduce the prettiest of their students or lure money from the wealthiest. It is, sadly, not always easy to resist these temptations and therefore we should keep the warnings about supernatural powers firmly in mind. White Tara warns us with these words:

> *Unfortunately, kundalini can be divorced from the love and bliss of your divine essence to a large degree and then it becomes extremely destructive. This is what people do who use black magic.*

Transformation of ordinary reality into paradise

In Tibetan Buddhism there is a teaching that has always deeply fascinated me. It says that once we reach higher states of awakening, our ordinary reality transforms into nirvana (loosely translated as paradise). This is described in the words, 'every sound is experienced as mantra and every person appears as a Buddha'.

It is important to understand that the experience of the world as paradise can happen anywhere – in a crowded city or in a deep, silent forest. Our perception of our surroundings changes so radically that we see only beauty where before we may have seen mundane reality or even ugliness. White Tara explained this dynamic to me like this:

When the blissful kundalini goes into your environment, it 'changes' it into the experience of a paradise. Everything pulsates in the same blissful rhythm. Every sense contact becomes an experience of ecstasy. You - including all of your perceptions - are all-pervading, blissful love. This process is accompanied by a perception of extreme beauty. This experience cannot be manufactured but happens on its own accord. It is called the 'pure view' or 'seeing the world as a paradise'.

Enlightenment

When kundalini is present we find that spiritual practices like prayer and meditation become deeply enjoyable thanks to the bliss we experience. We are able to dive more deeply into these practices and experience them as profoundly transformative and ultimately enlightening.

Tibetan Buddhism teaches that there are six higher practices which are necessary in order to reach enlightenment, called 'The Six Yogas of Naropa'. The first of these six practices is tummo, which is seen as the foundation of the five higher practices. In other words, kundalini is the most important prerequisite for achieving enlightenment.

According to these teachings, enlightenment can only be reached by uniting with a fully enlightened being – the deity. In the experience of this union our old sense of self is completely abandoned in favour of the divine sense of self of the deity. This practice is called deity-yoga. The Dalai Lama explains, 'In brief, the body of the Buddha is attained through meditating on it.' This is how White Tara describes the deity-state:

The deity-state is the full awareness of both of the two aspects of our divine essence – the sea of love and the life energy. You experience everything within your own heart because it expands infinitely. Other beings are simultaneously 'other' but they are also part of you. In practice, this means you 'are' a universe of love, and you invite other beings in, even if they suffer.

In the deity-state there is no ego but only love. A sense of ego only exists to make a distinction from others. When there is only love, there is no ego. However, in the deity-state you still feel like an individual and you never dissolve into nothingness or non-duality – or at least not for any length of time.

It is possible to experience first glimpses of enlightenment or deity-state relatively early in our meditation practice. But in order to stabilise this exalted state of mind we need to have the necessary energy, which is of course our kundalini energy. White Tara explained it to me like this:

> *If you can combine the deity-experience with kundalini in the abdomen, you manifest as the deity 'in the flesh' and only then can you also be recognised by others as the deity. We call this the 'manifested deity'. Without kundalini, the deity-state remains an internal meditation experience.*

Chapter three
Preparation for Awakening the Kundalini

This chapter is for both those who would like to prepare for a kundalini awakening and those who desire help to understand and integrate an involuntary awakening. If you are part of the second group, please use this chapter as a guideline to what you can do to make your kundalini awakening smoother.

First a little word of warning: For some people this preparation phase can take a long time, even years. But this time of preparation will be well spent and should not be seen as something that we should try to rush. Please take the following pieces of advice seriously because without them a kundalini awakening can be a difficult experience.

If we start the kundalini awakening too early it is like sending primary school children to a secondary school – it can be frightening and disconcerting. I myself would have loved the guidance that I will outline below and I hope that you will benefit from it, as well.

Generally speaking, the healthier we are and the more we are geared towards love and compassion, the better we are prepared for a kundalini awakening and the easier an existing kundalini process will be.

Seriously question your motivation for wanting to awaken your kundalini

Question yourself deeply about why you want to awaken the kundalini. You should only try to awaken the kundalini if you want to use it for the sole purpose of reaching enlightenment or union with God for the benefit of all beings. Any other aim, like having a more exciting sex-life, better health or wanting to attain supernatural powers will backfire because kundalini will make our life exceedingly painful unless we devote it entirely to our spiritual quest.

The best way to check your main motivation in life is to look at what you like doing outside of work and other obligations. Are you mainly looking to be fed or entertained by outside forces? Or do you love going within, exploring your own mind and engaging in spiritual practice?

You should only consider awakening your kundalini if you can answer 'yes' to the latter question. If you said 'yes' to the former question, you should devote yourself to a daily spiritual practice for at least a year before even considering awakening the kundalini.

Seriously consider the impact of a kundalini awakening

Remember all the changes that we have to make once kundalini is active, described in chapter two. Look at every point and ask yourself if you are ready – and more importantly – whether you are deeply interested in making all these changes in your life.

Do not assume that your kundalini awakening will be easy simply because your life has been easy so far. Nobody knows what is lurking in his or her unconscious mind, for the simple reason that it is, well, unconscious.

If you have already spent years in psychotherapy and spiritual practice, you will be better prepared than many but it is nevertheless important to take time to prepare yourself thoroughly.

Develop the right amount of willpower

In order for us to make the best of a kundalini awakening, our willpower needs to be like a well-tuned instrument – neither too weak, nor too strong. In order to check the state of your willpower, try to answer the following questions honestly:

Are you a thrill seeker, always looking for the next exciting thing?
Are you like a leaf in the wind, simply taking the easy path and going wherever your mood takes you?
Do you give in easily to temptation; do you eat or drink too much, or do you find it hard to resist other addictive tendencies?
Are you someone who finds it difficult to assert your needs and allows others to take advantage of you?
Do you tend to do what you like even if others get upset?
Are you too hard on yourself, drive yourself on relentlessly or do you often criticise yourself?
Do you sometimes feel hopeless and depressed and believe that you cannot reach your goals, no matter how hard you try?
Do you tend to overdo things, instead of working at a steady pace?

If you have answered 'yes' to any one of the first four questions your willpower may be a bit weak; a 'yes' to any of the second four questions may indicate that your willpower is a little too strong.

To succeed in awakening kundalini, we must be able to discipline ourselves and maintain a steady meditation practice but we also need to know when to stop and not be too hard on ourselves.

The best test of whether you have the right amount of willpower for a successful kundalini awakening is your ability to maintain a steady meditation practice that you are able to keep going no matter whether your life is stressful or happy. If you do not yet have a steady meditation practice, I suggest that you work with the preliminary practices outlined at the end of this chapter for at least a year on a daily basis before attempting to awaken your kundalini.

Use these preliminary exercises in two ways: firstly, develop the quality of mind that they are designed to achieve. Secondly, use the exercises to develop the right amount of willpower and self-discipline that is neither too weak, nor too strong.

Start dismantling your ego-defences

As we have seen in the previous chapter, the stripping away of our ego-defences is one of the main effects of awakened kundalini and even the most stable person will find themselves engulfed in rawness and sensitivity that at times can be difficult to bear. Here is a list of ego-defences that will not be at our disposal anymore, once our kundalini is awakened:

Ignoring our feelings
Rationalising our painful feelings away (e.g. trying hard to think positively)
Blaming others instead of taking responsibility for all our problems
Projecting our negativity on to outside 'enemies'
Believing that we are fine, instead of acknowledging our faults and weaknesses
Sweeping our conflicts with others under a rug
Believing that our childhood was totally fine, instead of acknowledging the many hurts that happen even to the most privileged children
Using food, drink, television etc. in order to repress our feelings
Taking ourselves very seriously
Believing that we ourselves are invulnerable and happy and that only other people have problems

The more we are able to dismantle these ego-defences *before* our kundalini awakens, the easier it will be once we are under the sway of this powerful energy. People who have spent time in psychotherapy or counselling have an advantage here because they have already developed the humility of acknowledging that their ego is not as faultless as they would wish.

It is those among us who had an easy ride in life, thus developing a strong self-belief, who may have the most problems once kundalini is awakened. This may seem counter-intuitive because in our society we equate a happy childhood with success in life. And while there certainly is a correlation on a mundane level, once kundalini is present it will mercilessly uncover any unrealistic ideas that we have about ourselves and, in that sense, enact the proverbial 'pride that comes before the fall'.

For instance, there are some popular spiritual teachings which suggest that all you need to do to is to 'be in the here and now' or that 'you are already enlightened' or that 'there is no path, nothing to do and no effort needed'. Anyone who has bought into these teachings will have a rather unpleasant awakening once their kundalini becomes active. Much to their dismay, these people will discover that these teachings are true only for the very last stages of the spiritual path but that for them the real work has not even begun.

In order to start dismantling your ego, try to humble yourself voluntarily: do the lowly work, serve others when you have the opportunity and humbly share your vulnerabilities with others instead of pretending that everything is fine. Be careful not to blame others for your problems, instead take responsibility for everything that is happening to you. This does not mean beating yourself up for everything negative that comes your way but rather developing a positive attitude towards yourself, just like a loving but firm parent.

Also, try to deal with your emotions more honestly and face up to your negativities and vulnerabilities. True spirituality is not about relentless positive thinking but about honesty, humility and compassion.

Finally, try taking yourself less seriously and laugh at yourself more often. Many stand-up comedians are very good at poking fun at their own insecurities and human weaknesses. These comedians are popular because, by laughing at themselves, they give us permission to take ourselves less seriously, as well. If you can poke fun at your own weaknesses like a stand-up comedian, you are making good headway in dismantling your ego.

Start diving into your unconscious mind

Kundalini will bring (often unpleasant) unconscious material into our conscious mind and that can be a blow for our ego if we have rigid ideas about how 'great', 'virtuous' or 'good' we are. For example, we may find ourselves thinking really nasty thoughts about others, which can be a bit shocking, initially. But we do not need to get upset about this because as long as we do not act on these thoughts, it is an essentially harmless but rather humbling experience. The more we can be open to this process by voluntarily diving into the darkness of our unconscious mind, the easier this process will be.

Yet again, people who have spent some time in psychotherapy are at an advantage here because they have already started to understand that a large proportion of their problems is due to decisions ruled by their unconscious, rather than their conscious and rational mind. Becoming aware of these unconscious beliefs and attitudes allows us to rectify immature decisions, superstitious attitudes and negative bias.

We can use various avenues to dive into our unconscious mind. The main road is of course meditation, which will allow us to gently and safely gain access to deeper layers of our mind. Other pathways include having deep and honest conversations about our feelings and motivations with someone we trust or simply spending plenty of quiet time in an undisturbed surrounding.

Make your life as healthy as possible

In order to withstand the impact of the kundalini, we should try to make every part of our life as healthy as possible. First of all, we should be able to stick to a healthy diet that consists largely of freshly prepared and nutritionally balanced meals. It is also important to avoid any form of extremes, such as no-carbohydrate or no-fat diets.

If we tend to overeat or have other forms of eating disorders, it is important to rectify the underlying stresses and anxieties that led to these patterns before engaging in awakening the kundalini. Remember that every problem, whether conscious or not, will be greatly amplified once kundalini is present. The way we eat is a mirror of how our mind works in general and therefore, adopting a balanced and healthy diet is good for our mind, as well as our body.

The next topic is sleep. Many people with awakened kundalini go through phases of sleep disturbances, which can be very taxing. So, it is advisable that you do not try to awaken your kundalini if you currently suffer from insomnia. Instead, you should try to focus on rectifying the stresses and problems that have led to the insomnia in the first place. Once you are sleeping better you will be much better prepared to withstand the onslaught of the kundalini.

If you are taking drugs, or if you used to take drugs, I strongly recommend that you wait at least three years of absolute clean living before considering awakening the kundalini. Be aware that many users of illegal drugs turn to alcohol once they stop taking them. Clean living means no illegal drugs and hardly any alcohol. It is okay to drink a glass of wine or beer on social occasions but it should only be one glass and it should be a rare occasion. Any regular alcohol consumption is counterproductive to a kundalini awakening and spiritual development in general.

I have noticed that there are a high percentage of former drug users among my kundalini clients. I cannot say whether this is due to the fact that more ex-drug users have kundalini awakenings or whether it is because ex-drug users have a harder time with their kundalini. In either case, these people have the double task of firstly dealing with the challenge of staying sober and secondly of dealing with all the challenges of their awakened kundalini.

Make your primary relationship as loving as possible

Kundalini will not allow us to get away with unhealthy patterns in relationships such as being overly submissive or domineering. All unresolved issues will burst open with great force once kundalini rises and if our primary relationship is in a bad state, we risk major upheavals or even a break-up.

Therefore, it is important to have our significant relationships at a level that is as loving and honest as possible. Ideally, your partner should be supportive of your spiritual and personal journey and you should be able to share with them what you are experiencing on a deep level.

Going through a kundalini awakening can sometimes feel like being in a pressure cooker and it would be nearly impossible to keep this process hidden from a partner who is unwilling or unable to talk about such issues. You will be much better prepared for this deep transformation if your primary relationship is in good shape.

Undo sexual repression

As we have seen in the first chapter, kundalini is sexual energy and more. So suppressing our sex-drive intensifies the pressure-cooker feelings of awakened kundalini. This can lead to many unnecessary problems. White Tara puts it like this:

> *You can't awaken kundalini if you are sexually repressed. This repression needs to be undone before we can start to awaken kundalini.*

It is advisable to do everything you can to develop a satisfying sexuality *before* you engage with something like a kundalini awakening. This can be achieved either by yourself through masturbation or with a loving partner.

I am aware that some people will need a lot of time to heal sexual problems and might also need a therapist to help them work through all their issues. But I think that this time will be well spent before opening up our inner energies. In order to clarify what a healthy sex life is, White Tara gives us this advice:

> *It is important to be happy and satisfied in all areas of your life, including your sexuality. Everything in your life should be done with love, so you should not be promiscuous or have sexual relations that are hurtful for anybody. Loving sex with your partner will actually enhance your kundalini experience and not lessen it. You should avoid any extreme, like withholding orgasms, unless you really feel like doing so.*

More traditional Hindu or Tibetan Buddhist approaches to awakening the kundalini advise celibacy and the avoidance of masturbation. The reasoning is that the sexual energy needs to be preserved so that we will have maximum energy for our kundalini awakening.

As we have seen, White Tara suggests a more moderate approach. I can only agree with her because I found that clients who refused to masturbate had the most debilitating kundalini symptoms.

Case-study: Arthur, 23 years

Arthur had participated in a workshop on tantric sexuality and had experienced a profound kundalini awakening as a result. Unfortunately, Arthur was not at all prepared for this awakening as he had visited the tantric workshop with the sole goal of finding a girlfriend, rather than embarking on a spiritual path.

Arthur had a long history of anxiety and compulsive thinking and he was absolutely terrified by the experience of sexual energy rising up his spine and body. He literally curled up into a ball of fear and anger (at the 'irresponsible' workshop leaders) and inwardly fought against these unwelcome sexual feelings. Unfortunately, it was exactly this resistance that made him focus more and more on these sexual feelings and this focus increased his sexual arousal. It was a vicious circle.

I urged Arthur to masturbate more often in order to let go of some of his pent up energy but he was too terrified to follow my advice. For some reason he believed that masturbation would increase his sexual charge.

Eventually, after several months of encouragement, Arthur followed my advice to masturbate and experienced a dramatic lessening of his sexual energy and kundalini symptoms. We also worked on his anxiety with an anti-anxiety technique. Simultaneously, I tried my best to reassure Arthur that these feelings in his body were not dangerous. Very gradually Arthur calmed down and learnt to make peace with his kundalini.

Heal low self-esteem and excessive self-criticism

It is not a good idea to have a kundalini awakening if you suffer from low self-esteem and are prone to excessive self-criticism. We need to have a gentle relationship with ourselves and ideally we should relate to ourselves as if we are our own best friends. It is particularly important to refrain from speaking harshly to ourselves.

If you have this problem, the following exercise can help you to rectify it. You can also refer to my book 'The Five-Minute Miracle' for more in-depth explanations.

Exercise: Learning to love yourself

Pray to your higher power for help to love yourself.

See loving light coming from your higher power enveloping you in a bubble of light that envelops you like a blanket of love.

Tune in to the love of your higher power and wish yourself to be happy and healed, as if you were your own best friend.

Alternatively, think about someone you find easy to like and love. Deeply wish this person to be happy and healed. Once you feel this warm emotion, simply turn it on to yourself without changing it. Wish yourself to be happy and healed just like you wished this for your friend or family member. Include all your problems and weaknesses in your loving intention.

The love you feel for yourself should feel like the love a parent gives to their child. It is like giving yourself an inner hug with a blanket of loving, healing light.

Do this exercise every day until it becomes second nature.

Forgive everyone who has hurt you

An important part of preparing yourself for a kundalini awakening is letting go of all conscious and half-conscious resentments that are festering away in the recesses of your mind. Just like all other unresolved issues, these resentments will be greatly amplified once kundalini is present and can lead to a lot of upset. So, it is best to let go of these grudges before the kundalini awakens.

> **Exercise: Letting go of all your resentments**
>
> **Make** a list of everyone who has ever hurt you. Focus particularly on parents, carers, family members and ex-partners.
>
> **Pray** to your higher power for help to forgive everyone.
>
> **See** loving light coming from your higher power enveloping you in a bubble of light like a blanket of love. Tune in to the love of your higher power and wish yourself to be happy and healed, as if you were your own best friend. Include all your problems and weaknesses in your loving wish.
>
> **Picture** one of the people who have hurt you in your inner eye and see them enveloped by a bubble of loving light just like yourself.
>
> **Tell** that person what they have done wrong. Then say, 'what you have done is wrong but I now will stop any further grudges against you and I wish you to be happy and healed'. Imagine that if this person was happy and healed, they would immediately regret what they have done and start a path of self-healing to deal with the issues that led to their wrong-doing.
>
> **If you wish** to have a complete separation from this person, let them drift away in their bubble until it has disappeared beyond the horizon.
>
> **Repeat** this exercise for 14 days or until you feel that your resentments have completely turned into compassion.
>
> **If you are** still in contact with the person who has hurt you, try to communicate to them about your hurt feelings and also about your forgiveness.
>
> **Work** in this way with every person from your list.

Heal chronic depression, anxiety, pain and fatigue

If you suffer from chronic depression, anxiety, pain and fatigue, it would be much wiser to heal these issues before starting to awaken the kundalini. If you were to have a kundalini awakening while still suffering from these problems, it would only aggravate them.

You may use the process of higher-consciousness healing that I have explained in my book The Five-Minute Miracle to heal these problems or find a suitable therapist.

In my counselling practice I have found that most forms of depression, chronic pain and fatigue are caused by repressed anger. Once you have acknowledged your deep-seated resentments, you can use the forgiveness exercise from the section above. It is sometimes necessary to communicate with the person who caused your anger and find a way to negotiate better compromises.

Let go of the desire for wealth, fame and admiration

If your life is governed by a desire for wealth, fame and admiration you will find it very difficult to awaken the kundalini. In order to awaken the kundalini, your main desire needs to be directed on to your spiritual development, your higher power or simply on wanting to love and help others.

If you do not have these deep desires, it is important to reflect on the impermanence of wealth, fame and admiration and also on the fact that none of these things can bring us lasting happiness.

Make your life morally impeccable

Morality does not have such a good name nowadays because many people associate it with unnecessary repression. But morality will never be unnecessary because it simply means living a life of honesty and love. In a nutshell, all moral rules boil down to the golden rule of treating others in the way we want to be treated ourselves - like keeping all of our promises and telling the truth.

Many forms of behaviour that are somewhat permissible in our society are not honest and loving; for example, having affairs or disowning children. Sadly, I personally know a Buddhist teacher who has a child from a one-night-stand who he has never acknowledged and sees nothing wrong with this situation. If his kundalini awakened, he would probably suffer terrible guilt-feelings for neglecting his daughter so badly.

It is therefore important to make our life morally impeccable now and make amends wherever possible. This will also help us to withstand the temptation of ego-inflation that may occur when kundalini awakens. Unfortunately, there are many people who have failed to withstand this temptation and have abused their kundalini powers for their own selfish needs. Simply searching the Internet with the keywords 'kundalini teacher' and 'scandal' will bring up a shocking number of spiritual teachers who have lost their moral integrity once they achieved greater personal power after their kundalini awakening. The more moral integrity we develop now, the easier it will be to avoid this danger.

Develop a devoted relationship with the divine

Tibetan Buddhism teaches that we cannot reach enlightenment solely by ourselves, no matter how much kundalini we have, and that we need the grace of a deity to finally reach enlightenment. It is therefore important to have a devoted relationship to a divine being or an enlightened master. White Tara explains:

> *Your life is one long preparation to unite with a divine being and this union is the goal of the kundalini awakening. Kundalini is driving you on to seek this union.*

So, White Tara is saying that the union with the divine is the purpose of a kundalini awakening and that it does not make sense to awaken the kundalini without this goal. She also points out that we need the support of a divine being during a kundalini awakening:

> *You need a relationship with a divine being because sometimes the impact of the kundalini can be overwhelming and frightening. You need to have this protection of a divine being during these times. Nobody else can help you when you feel that way.*

Some people who are engaged in a path of meditation have a conscious or unconscious desire to become independent and free from the need for other people, a teacher or even the divine. This need for independence is unhealthy because we all need others – other human beings and also a divine being. If we cannot own up to these needs, we do not understand our basic human nature and this lack of humility will lead to difficulties once the kundalini is awakened. White Tara says:

> *You can't be without relationships. The sole reason for your existence is to relate to others and express your love to them or be awakened by them to higher states of love and bliss. This giving and receiving of love is part of our intrinsic nature and gives us most satisfaction.*

Our higher power can be one of the well-known figures of a traditional religion or it can be a more personal sense of a higher power. Some people call this power Source, Goddess or Higher Consciousness. No matter which name we choose or what religion we follow, the divine should have the following qualities:

The divine is a living being or not just an abstract quality.
The divine being is the source of highest love, wisdom and purest life force and balances these qualities of our divine nature perfectly.
The divine being dearly loves you and wants you to be happy, healed and spiritually evolved.

Some people have a problem with the concept of the Christian God who is said to have created the world and guides us and interferes in our life. This is not the Buddhist concept of our higher power that I am using in this book. A Buddhist deity has not created the world but the world has been created by the people who live in it - as we have already discussed. Also, a Buddhist deity cannot interfere in people's lives and give or withhold help like the Christian God. The Buddhist idea of a deity is more like a loving presence who serves as an emotional and spiritual model and support.

How to develop a devoted relationship to the divine
If you already have a devoted relationship to a divine being, you can skip the next few paragraphs and directly go to the next section. But if you do not yet have this relationship, here are a few tips on how to develop and deepen one.

I assume that everybody who has read this book up to this stage has strong spiritual inclinations and at least the willingness to have a deeper relationship with a divine being. In order to nurture this relationship you simply need to give it more attention. Talk to God or your higher power like a friend. Tell him or her all your worries and humbly ask for help.

You don't need to have faith in a higher power to start this practice. Simply by talking to your divine being your belief will grow on its own accord. I have read somewhere an inspiring statement that for every step you make towards God, he will make ten steps towards you. In other words, the presence of a divine being will make itself known in your mind as soon as you develop the willingness to receive his or her blessing. I have found this to be true in my own life.

Develop witness consciousness

I already talked at length about the fact that our awareness will expand once kundalini is awakened and that we may be confronted with all sorts of unusual phenomena. These phenomena may range from surfacing of childhood traumas, to past life experiences, experiencing the contents of other people's minds or paranormal visions or a variety of spiritual experiences.

It cannot be overstated how important it is that we are well prepared for this development and an important way to get ready is to develop witness consciousness. Witness consciousness is the ability to *watch* or *observe* the contents of our mind from the viewpoint of a calm and impartial 'witness', instead of identifying with whatever is going on in our mind and being swept away by it. White Tara says:

> *You need to have a great interest in your inner life and not shy away from your darker sides and strong emotions. For that you need the ability to watch your emotions rather than identifying with them.*

Through witness consciousness we can learn to have a tiny little distance between ourselves and our thoughts, inner images and emotions so that they do not dominate us. This allows us a greater choice in responding to the challenges in our life. Instead of knee-jerk responses to every provocation, we will gradually become able to *choose* our responses more wisely.

White Tara also makes the point that we need to be more than a passive observer and be really interested in our inner life. Unfortunately, I have seen in some of my clients that it is possible to practice witness consciousness but remain largely unconscious, nevertheless. If we are afraid of discovering aspects in ourselves that are incompatible with our positive self-image, we will find a subtle way to repress this material while outwardly pretending to do the opposite.

In other words, witness consciousness only really makes sense if we have a courageous and interested attitude towards ourselves and if we want to dive down into the depths of our being and deal with whatever we may find – whether it is flattering to our ego or not.

Exercise: Develop witness consciousness
Sit down and start focusing on your breath. Don't alter your breath but simply observe how it is flowing in and out.

> ***Start observing*** your thoughts, emotions and body sensations in the same way as you observe your breath – as an impartial non-interfering witness. Do not try to change or manipulate the contents of your mind but simply observe.
> ***Do not fixate*** rigidly on what you observe but stay relaxed. Allow your thoughts, emotions and body sensations to appear but also to leave your mind again.
> ***If your mind*** starts to wander, notice this without judgement and simply bring your mind back to your breath and your witness consciousness.
> ***Develop*** a steady practice of witness consciousness for at least 15 minutes a day while sitting upright and with your eyes half-open.
> ***Get into a habit*** of observing your thoughts and emotions during all waking hours.

Dedicate your life to the development of love

The sole purpose of our spiritual and personal development is to have so much love that we can be of real benefit to others. The importance of having this altruistic motivation cannot be overstated. It is therefore of paramount importance that we always practice loving kindness alongside our kundalini-awakening practice. White Tara explains the necessity in this way:

> *Kundalini is the force that brings your lower passions into your awareness and love is the remedy that heals these passions. Therefore, you always need love and kundalini together and not only one quality.*

The following meditation is a Tibetan Buddhist practice, which is called 'The Immeasurable'. It can be found in many different variants and it includes the meditations of loving yourself and forgiving everybody, which we have discussed earlier. It is equally important for those who want to prepare for a kundalini awakening and for those who wish to alleviate symptoms of an existing kundalini arousal.

> **Exercise: Develop loving-kindness**
> ***Pray*** to your higher power for help to love yourself and others.
> ***See*** loving light coming from your higher power enveloping you in a bubble of light like a blanket of love. Tune in to the love of your higher power and wish yourself to be happy and healed as if you were your own best friend.
> ***Think*** about someone you find easy to like and love. Deeply wish this person to

be happy and healed and see them enveloped with white light. Once you feel this warm feeling, simply turn the white loving light on to yourself without changing it. Wish yourself to be happy and healed just like you wished this for the other person. The loving feeling for yourself should feel like a loving parent loves their child. It is like giving yourself an inner hug with a blanket of loving healing light. Love yourself, including all your problems and weaknesses.

Think about someone you feel neutral about, like a shop assistant or a stranger in the street. Envelop this person with the same intensity of love and white light just as you did with your favourite person and yourself. See them enveloped in a bubble of loving light and wish them to be happy and healed from the bottom of your heart. If you find it difficult to muster the intensity of feeling, try to imagine all the suffering that this person may have gone through or imagine that this person could be your own parent or child.

Think about a person who has caused you to suffer in some way. Wish this person to be happy and healed in exactly the same way as you have done before with yourself, your favourite person and the person you feel neutral about. Imagine that if the person who has hurt you were happy and healed, they would immediately regret their wrongdoing and wish you to be happy in return. If you find it difficult to muster the intensity of feelings, try to imagine that the other person has behaved in this uncaring and hurtful way because they were suffering. Nobody who is truly happy would try to hurt other people. Try to have compassion for the suffering of the other person and wish them to be happy and healed.

Think about a well-known historical figure that has brought great suffering to many people - for example a dictator. Imagine the terrible suffering that this person must have experienced to build up a motivation to be so brutal and cruel to others. Feel compassion and wish this person to be happy and healed just like the other people in your earlier meditation. Imagine that this person deeply repents their wrongdoing and vows to better their ways.

Imagine loving light spreading out all over your hometown, bringing happiness and healing to all people living there.

Imagine loving light spreading out all over your country, bringing happiness and healing to all people living there.

Imagine loving light spreading out all over the earth, bringing happiness and healing to all people.

Finally, imagine loving light spreading out all over the universe, bringing comfort

> and healing to all beings.

When practising this loving-kindness meditation, you do not need to go through every step every time you meditate. However, you should always start with loving yourself because we cannot truly love others as long as we reject parts of ourselves.

Get acquainted to the idea of non-self

According to Tibetan Buddhism, all our suffering comes from the illusory idea of having a personal ego that we need to protect and defend at any price. The best way to understand this problem is to remember a time when you felt deeply insulted and humiliated. If you are like most people, you felt angry, upset and somehow 'injured'. There is a sense that someone invaded your territory and that you could not protect 'yourself' from this attack. But what exactly were you trying to protect? The Buddhist answer to this question is 'nothing'.

Obviously, we feel that we are trying to defend 'ourselves', but when we actually look for this 'self', it cannot be found anywhere. It is not in our arms, legs, stomach, chest or head. If we opened any part of our body we could not find our 'self' anywhere. This concept is referred to as 'emptiness' in Tibetan Buddhism – we are 'empty' of an inherent self.

If we fully realise emptiness, we will experience our inner being as the blissful spacious experience of our divine nature, which has no core and no boundaries, stretching out infinitely. In this experience all our fears and angers will cease. After all, if there is no ego that we need to protect but only loving blissful space, there is no reason to get upset about being humiliated or criticised.

A full realisation of this all-important state of mind can only be achieved through the awakening of the kundalini. Without the flow of this strong and blissful energy we may understand the idea of non-self theoretically but it will not stop our negative emotions. Nevertheless, it is important to make a start into this investigation because clinging to the idea of having a personal ego causes so much suffering.

The following exercise is a classic Buddhist meditation that will help you to investigate this interesting topic. Make sure that you approach this exercise purely from an experiential perspective and not in an intellectual or theoretical way.

> **Exercise: Investigate your ego**
> **Ask** yourself what part of your body is your 'self': your head, heart or stomach, for example.
> **If you have** a feeling that your self resides in a particular part of your body, mentally go within this body part and try to find this self. You will not find it anywhere.
> **Repeat** the exercise while remembering a time when you were deeply insulted or humiliated. Yet again, you will not be able to find this illusive ego, even though you feel it so keenly in a moment of humiliation.

The idea of emptiness or non-self used to confuse me a great deal (as I think it confuses many people) because in my work with wives of alcoholic husbands I was always trying to strengthen the ego of these women. I would say to them, 'you deserve a good life; stand up against your abusive husband, do not allow him to walk all over you,' and so on. I just could not understand how this advice fitted in with the idea of non-self that is so central in Tibetan Buddhism.

The answer to this conundrum is resolved through the doctrine of the 'two truths'. According to Tibetan Buddhism, there are two truths that co-exist, even though they seem to be contradictory. The first truth is the absolute truth, in which we realise the emptiness of our divine nature as infinitely blissful and loving space without core or boundaries.

The second truth is called the 'relative truth' and it states that we also exist as ordinary people – as 'me' and 'you'- and that we need to be skilful at that level too in order to have clear communication and good relationships. My experience is that Tibetan Buddhism excels at explaining and achieving the absolute truth and that Western psychology excels at the level of the relative truth.

Some spiritual practitioners believe that being on a spiritual path means that they do not need to deal with the psychological side of themselves and that realising the absolute truth will take care of it all. Unfortunately, that is not my personal experience and I do not see this happening in my students, either. I have met a number of meditation practitioners who have frequent glimpses of the absolute truth, yet their lack of skill in relationships and communication draws them back over and over again into ego-games, with all the suffering that goes with them.

On our path to enlightenment we need clear ego-boundaries and the ability to deal with others without manipulation, domination or unhealthy submissiveness. Once we have achieved this, the way is clear to dive deeply into the bliss of the absolute truth and stabilise our mind for longer periods in this exalted state.

Have a safety net in place

The final point I want to make is that you should know where to turn if you run into trouble. In the good old days, teachings about awakening the kundalini were kept secret and were only given to devoted students of a qualified guru. There are good arguments for this line of approach as it is not always easy to come to terms with the many changes the kundalini forces us to make and also because there is a danger of abusing the power of the kundalini for selfish ends.

However, as I have already told you, White Tara has asked me to make her teachings about the kundalini available to others and after resisting for several years I have now accepted this task. My opinion has been swayed by the sight of so much misinformation about kundalini on the Internet. So many of my clients are terribly afraid after reading all sorts of horror stories and it sometimes takes several sessions before I can manage to reassure them that a kundalini awakening is not the horror trip that they imagine it to be.

Having said all that, a kundalini awakening can throw up many challenges and for that reason I strongly advise that you find out who to contact in case of difficulty *before* you start to awaken the kundalini.

Ideally, you should have a supportive person in your life with whom you can freely talk about spiritual and psychological topics and who you trust enough to reveal the most intimate experiences you have. This could be your partner, a friend or a therapist. This person does not need to understand everything about kundalini but they should not be opposed to this idea and be generally supportive of your spiritual journey. In an ideal world, you should also have a spiritual teacher or kundalini therapist who can guide you and help you if things go wrong.

If you do not have such a friend, teacher or therapist, you should ask yourself earnestly whether the time is right for you to awaken your kundalini. Ask yourself why you do not have such a friend and whether you are striving for too much independence. It would be wiser to first work on your relationships before engaging on the path of the kundalini.

Chapter four
Purification of the Chakras

Chakra awakening is the bridge between our preparatory exercises and the actual kundalini awakening. In fact, purifying our chakras is already a mild form of kundalini awakening and at the same time it will make it easier to meet the preparatory conditions outlined in the previous chapter. Therefore, chakra purification can be practiced simultaneously with the preparatory exercises.

Chakra work will also help you to alleviate your symptoms if you have had an involuntary awakening. But please proceed slowly and with caution. As soon as your symptoms become worse, back off from chakra practices and simply focus on witness consciousness and loving-kindness practices for another month or two. White Tara says:

> *The most important preparation for a kundalini awakening is that all your chakras need to be completely blissful and that you have a loving motivation.*

What are the chakras?

Chakras are energy centres in our body – places at which we will feel the life force in the form of positive and negative emotions and physical sensations. Once our kundalini is awakened, these sensations can become very strong and at times overwhelming. But even without awakened kundalini, most people feel sexual arousal in their abdominal chakra and love in their heart chakra, while thoughts appear to be in their head chakra.

There are many different chakra systems in the various esoteric traditions around the world. The Hindu system is the most well known and recognises seven main chakras: in the top of the skull, forehead, throat, chest, solar plexus, navel and lower abdomen. The Taoist system speaks of only three main chakras: in the head, chest and abdomen (called the three tan tiens) and the Tibetan Buddhist system recognises five main chakras: in the head, throat, chest, higher abdomen and lower abdomen. White Tara spoke to me mostly about the five main chakras of the Tibetan system but also referred to the seven main chakras of the Hindu system.

Every thought, every emotion and every physical movement or sensation is registered by energetic changes in our chakras. For the sake of simplicity, I will call all unpleasant thoughts and feelings a 'blocked chakra' and all pleasant sensations an 'open or purified chakra'. In reality, however, nothing gets 'blocked' or 'opened' - we simply perceive the distorted or purified life force in one of the chakras.

When all our chakras are completely purified, we achieve enlightenment. The first signs of movement in this direction are intense feelings of bliss combined with great insight into the nature of reality. As we have learnt in the first chapter, the life force only ever appears in conjunction with the sea of love, which feels like endlessly open and accepting space. So, once a chakra is open it is experienced as an endless expanse of sparkling bliss that arises from and surrounds a certain chakra.

In order to stabilise this bliss and also the accompanying wisdom, we need the energy of kundalini. In other words, people without kundalini can experience short moments of ecstasy (as in an orgasm, for example) but in order to stabilise this bliss and reach enlightenment, we need awakened kundalini. White Tara explains:

> Chakras are the essence of your being. There is no distinction between the feeling in a chakra and yourself. In the heart you are love if your chakra is purified, or hatred, if your chakra is blocked. And in the head you are your blissful vision if your chakra is purified, or your negative thoughts if your chakra is blocked. When you start working with the chakras it may feel as if you and the chakra are distinct but that is only a transient illusion.

> The chakras are the entry points to your divine essence. The various blissful vibrations of your divine essence are experienced in the different chakras just like differently coloured rays of light: in the head chakra you feel bliss, in the throat chakra joy, in the heart chakra love, in the solar plexus chakra peace and in the abdominal chakra power and pleasure.

Chakra change means life change

White Tara goes on to explain that the life force emerging from our chakras creates our reality and that changing our chakras means changing our life. I find this teaching most exciting as it shows a way to change our entire life simply by focusing on a single chakra. Instead of trying the change the myriad of things and people that surround us, we are shown the short-cut of changing the state of our chakra and by doing so our entire life will change accordingly. I can vouch from my own experience that this life change through chakra work is not only a theory but really works in the most amazing way. In my life story in chapter five I will tell you more details of how this happened. The process of creation and life-change will be more powerful the more kundalini we have at our disposal. White Tara says:

> The seven different vibrations in the different chakras are the building blocks of all phenomena. The world you see around you is a direct projection of the sum of vibrations in your combined chakras.

> From your divine essence in your chakras whole universes emerge like images from a projector – good or bad. Your chakra is the projector, your feelings and thoughts are the slide and the kundalini is the light that projects the image of the slide into the outside world. The more purified your chakras are, the more beautiful your world will appear.

> The heart is the most important chakra and all chakras support the heart. It is from here that your deepest wishes arise and then take form as images in the head through the finest vibration of the life force and finally gain physical reality through the kundalini in the navel.

I cannot emphasise enough how important chakra work is to change and improve our entire life, starting from our emotional wellbeing, to our health, our relationships, our finances, success in our career and finally to our spiritual enlightenment. In White Tara's words:

> In its unopened state a chakra either feels numb, painful or full of frequent negative emotions. It spawns a succession of seemingly unrelated problems in your health, relationships, surroundings and emotional wellbeing. For example, a blocked solar plexus chakra could cause stomach pain, noise sensitivity, noisy neighbours, worry and fear. The one thing that links all these problems is the blocked solar plexus chakra. Once this chakra is opened, all these problems disappear.

I can attest to the fact that all this is true because the teaching of White Tara was given to me because I suffered from all of these problems myself. Just as she predicted, all these problems disappeared once I had worked with my solar plexus chakra and was able to open it. White Tara also explains how we can use chakra work in order to create the life of our dreams:

> *Chakras are like keys that unlock the entrance to the world that you want to live in. The more you focus on a particular chakra with bliss, the more its particular quality will manifest in your life.*

I can attest to the fact that these teachings actually work not only by looking at my own life but also at the lives of my clients. For example, I have seen how the opening of the navel chakra has resulted in doubling and even quadrupling of someone's income, and how the opening of the heart chakra resulted in the manifesting of a true soulmate relationship. But White Tara cautions us to avoid the flawed belief that we alone create our entire universe. She says:

> *You do not live in an entirely self-created universe. Improving the vibrations in your chakras – and with them your world – happens when you unite with more loving and happier beings.*

So, it is crucial to understand that we can only improve the state of our chakras through loving contact with someone else whose chakras are at a higher vibration. By offering deep devotion and love to this being, we become able to adopt their higher vibrations for ourselves. And once we have stabilised these higher vibrations within ourselves, we will see them manifesting in our outside world over time.

For many people all this may appear rather esoteric and removed from their everyday experience. But as a psychotherapist I am in the privileged position of seeing this dynamic play out in all of my clients. Here is just one example of the profound effect of chakra work, which I have witnessed in many variations in many different clients over the years. I have merged some of these cases, so that the dynamic will become clearer. This is an example about someone who wanted to improve the state of her relationships but it equally works with improving our spiritual realisations.

Case-study: Natalie, 42 years
Natalie was at a very low ebb when she came to see me. After a divorce and several failed relationships to unloving men she just could not imagine ever finding a loving husband.

On closer inspection it turned out that Natalie thought very negatively about herself (blocked head chakra) and tended to over-reciprocate every little favour from a new potential partner in the early stages of the relationship (blocked throat chakra). She was also quite incapable of voicing her needs to a partner and caved in as soon as there was the slightest power struggle (blocked throat chakra and navel chakra). Due to some deep-seated self-loathing, Natalie felt she did not deserve love (blocked heart-chakra) and to top off her miserable condition, Natalie also suffered from severe anxiety (blocked solar plexus chakra). Finally, Natalie had trouble with her root chakra as well, which manifested in the inability to find sexual satisfaction.

In my work with Natalie, I first helped her to get over the block to loving herself, therefore unblocking her heart chakra. Once she could love herself, it was relatively easy for Natalie to remove the overly negative ideas she held about herself (open head chakra). As a result, she became able to voice her needs more confidently in subsequent blind dates with potential partners (open throat chakra). I also showed Natalie the anti-anxiety breathing technique, which greatly pacified her solar plexus chakra and allowed her to come off her anxiety medication.

We then role-played arguments that she had had with her ex-husband over child-care, which strengthened Natalie's power - allowing her to assert herself much more forcefully than before (open throat and navel chakra).

After a year of doing this work, Natalie met a very attractive man who was very different from anybody she had dated before. He was loving and attentive and Natalie embarked on a beautiful relationship with him (open heart chakra). To her great amazement she felt truly loved for the first time in her adult life. She was even able to enjoy sex more than she had done before (open root chakra) due to her partner's loving attentiveness and her own fresh confidence in voicing her needs (open throat chakra).

A year later, she and her partner moved in together to a peaceful house in the country allowing Natalie to leave behind her noisy flat in the big city that she had never liked (open solar plexus chakra). Natalie was also able to fulfil yet another of her heart desires, which was to give up her employed job and start her own business. After a year of hard work, she became quite successful in her new line of work (open navel chakra).

Two years after starting to work with me, Natalie's life had entirely changed due to the raising of the vibrations in all her chakras.

White Tara explains the dynamic outlined in this case study in these words:

> *Suffering occurs when you lose contact with the pure divine vibrations in a chakra and experience cruder vibrations. This is usually triggered by the experience of someone rejecting your love. As a result, your chakras develop an unhealthy range of vibrations, which then spawn a multitude of problems on the emotional, physical and relationship levels. These problems will keep coming and coming until you fix their root problem, which is the state of vibration in your chakra.*

It is interesting to note that White Tara says that most suffering arises from the experience of rejected love. This may have happened in our childhood, in the course of a difficult love relationship, or it may even have happened in a former life. It is this experience of rejected love that leads to a multitude of negative attitudes and emotions like anger, jealousy, pride, envy, fear and depression, which in turn can affect our physical health and our entire life. When I asked White Tara what to do about this all-pervading problem, she gave me this succinct advice:

> *The challenge is to leave your chakras open despite feeling rejected and to send positive energy to others, no matter whether or not others give you love and energy.*

So, White Tara points us yet again to the main solution to all our problems, which is to become more loving, even in the face of adversity and rejection.

The central channel

Now things start to become a bit more complicated. According to many esoteric schools around the world, including Tibetan Buddhism, our chakras are connected through an energetic channel, which is called the central channel. The teachings say that this channel runs alongside or inside the spine and needs to be purified in order for the kundalini to flow more freely. White Tara has an interesting perspective on this dynamic. She explains:

> *All energetic changes in the chakras are registered in the head chakra because it is the most sensitive of all chakras. Therefore, you always feel the bliss of an open chakra and the head chakra simultaneously. When this*

feedback loop becomes faster and stronger, a line appears. This line is the central channel.

The central channel is not really a channel and you can't move energy in it. It is more like a holographic image that arises when the bliss of kundalini is strong. The further the chakra is away from the brain, the stronger the line appears. Therefore, the traditional idea of kundalini rising up the spine is not true. What happens is that the lower chakras become purified.

Once all chakras are open, the central channel spontaneously appears as a white, warm and blissful glowing egg with its widest point at the heart level. The top, middle and bottom end look like suns.

The central channel is often experienced in the spine. Once you have been accustomed to the vibration in the spine, you can try to feel it in the middle of your body. It will become more tangible.

I can confirm that any pleasant sensation in a chakra seems to 'rise up' to the brain and brings about a similar sensation in our head. The important point to understand here is that this sensation of energy 'rising' is not real. It is just a sensation that happens spontaneously once a lower chakra is purified and therefore we should refrain from trying to manufacture this experience.

When I first learnt to work consciously with the kundalini, I made the mistake of thinking that the central channel was a real hollow tube through which I could send energy. So, I mentally tried to 'push' energy up and down this imagined channel. As a result, I always developed unpleasant side effects, which quickly spoiled any pleasant sensation I had at the beginning.

It took me a while to fully understand that any mental effort or manipulation technique is counter-productive when it comes to energy work. The deepest nature of our chakras is identical with our divine nature, which is the perfect balance of the sea of love and life energy. The sea of love is a sense of total relaxation, openness and allowing. It is not compatible with any form of mental effort. Therefore, by trying to push or manipulate the energy we will always fall out of our divine nature and go right into our negative emotions, like frustration that things are not working or worry that we may not be doing it right. Instead, the emphasis needs to be on allowing and surrendering to what happens naturally.

What each chakra represents

The following descriptions of the chakras look at five categories: location; core function; open chakra, chakra filled with kundalini, and closed chakra. As explained before, an open chakra refers to a high-functioning and purified chakra and a closed chakra indicates a malfunctioning chakra that produces negative feelings and symptoms. A closed chakra will also create illnesses in the organs surrounding the chakra and foster negative life circumstances.

'Chakra filled with kundalini' describes what will happen to us once we are able to stabilise the heightened energy of kundalini in a chakra. Generally speaking, when we have sufficient kundalini in a chakra we gain the ability to manifest its qualities. For example, an 'open throat chakra' indicates a feeling of joy in our throat and it also indicates the ability to communicate positively with others. If the throat chakra is 'filled with sufficient kundalini', we may become able to write a book that becomes a bestseller or become a public speaker who is extremely successful.

The more kundalini we have in a chakra, the greater our ability to influence others and manifest our dreams. In other words, if we have sufficient kundalini in all our chakras, we can form loving bonds with a huge number of people and inspire them to develop love in themselves. The great saints of human history are examples of this wonderful development.

Crown

Location: In the Tibetan system the crown and forehead are two aspects of the same chakra and can be felt in the middle of the brain. The Hindu system recognises two distinct head chakras: the forehead chakra between the eyebrows, and the crown chakra, found at the top of the skull.

Core function: This chakra determines how we relate to our higher power and whether we believe in spiritual and metaphysical phenomena or have a purely materialistic outlook.

Open crown chakra: Heavenly bliss – a feeling that you are connected to and supported by something bigger than yourself - to your heavenly parents. It is a profound feeling of not being alone in the universe, of being guided, loved and protected by higher beings. You feel like you are in paradise.

With kundalini: Genuine visions and real-life encounters with divine beings

Closed crown chakra: Depression, atheism, nihilism, materialism, a feeling of being unsupported by higher powers, fear of dying, diseases in and around the head

Forehead

Location: In the Tibetan system the crown and forehead are two aspects of the same chakra and can be felt in the middle of the brain. The Hindu system recognises two distinct head chakras - the forehead chakra between the eyebrows and the crown chakra, found at the top of the skull. (The eyes themselves do not belong to the forehead chakra but to the heart chakra.)

Core function: This chakra determines our outlook on life: what we believe and understand and how motivated we are to learn. It also determines how much awareness we have, or whether we strive for unawareness through mind-numbing activities.

Open forehead chakra: Ability to visualise and to learn fast, bliss from positive views, optimism and wisdom, insight and ability to see things positively

With kundalini: Clairvoyance, wisdom about the nature of reality and brilliant ideas

Closed forehead chakra: Depression, negative views, materialism, pessimism, hopelessness, inability or unwillingness to learn and memorise, and diseases in and around the head

Throat

Location: In the middle of the throat

Core function: The throat chakra determines how confident we are in communicating and expressing ourselves and also how we exchange ideas and goods. You give, receive and swap through this chakra. You may use money in the process but the amount of money you have is determined by your navel chakra.

Open throat chakra: Joy and confidence in communication, positive reciprocal exchange of goods and services that enrich and bring joy to both parties. People trust your words.

With kundalini: Numerous people will listen to what you say and believe in you. Abundant giving and receiving that is always fair.

Closed throat chakra: Stress, fear, shyness, meanness, fear of public speaking, problems with communication, isolation, poverty, stress, greed, untrustworthiness, more giving than receiving or trying to take more than you are willing to give, diseases in and around the throat

Heart

Location: In the middle of the chest

Core function: The heart is the seat of our innermost being – the place we identify with most deeply. All impulses - pure and impure - originate from the heart and therefore the state of the heart chakra determines essentially how much overall happiness, love and freedom we can experience. The state of the heart chakra determines the strength of our will to live and how much we wish to unite in love with others. It governs loving relationships, including marriage and parent-child relationships. The heart chakra is the most vulnerable of all the chakras, where we take 'everything to heart' or can even be 'heart-broken'.

Open heart chakra: Profound feelings of love, happiness and compassion, ability to unite in love with others and live in loving relationship

With kundalini: Union with our higher power and manifestation as the deity (reaching enlightenment)

Closed heart chakra: Emotional hurt, loneliness, rejection, meanness, hatred, cruelty, lack of love relationships and diseases in and around the chest

Solar plexus

Location: Just below the rib-cage

Core function: The solar-plexus chakra determines our ability to trust and to experience peace and harmony in our lives.

Open solar-plexus chakra: Deep peace, trust and freedom from fear, serenity, equanimity – even in noisy, hectic and threatening surroundings

With kundalini: Ability to create very peaceful, safe and harmonious relationships and surroundings

Closed solar plexus chakra: Fear, anxiety, worry, lack of faith, over-sensitivity, relationships and surroundings in which we are stressed, frightened and unable to trust, diseases in and around the stomach, liver, gallbladder, pancreas and spleen

Navel

Location: In the Tibetan Buddhist system the navel and root chakra can be visualised together anywhere between the perineum and the navel – wherever we feel most energy. In the Hindu system the navel chakra is located slightly below the navel and the root chakra sits in our perineum.

Core function: The navel chakra is the seat of the kundalini and once it is opened, this powerful energy will start to flow. The flow of the kundalini increases the vibrations of all other chakras and acts like a bridge to the tangible world by giving us the power to manifest our desires in the physical universe. It is for this reason that the navel chakra can lead us most astray from our spiritual path and should only be opened when all other chakras are blissful and we are firmly grounded in a path of altruistic love. If we open the navel chakra prematurely, it will amplify all negative feelings and egotistical impulses in the other chakras.

Open navel chakra: Intense pleasure, unshakable confidence, excited joy, enthusiasm, energy and ability to assert yourself, feeling of strength and power

With kundalini: Powerful ability to change ourselves, our environment and other people and to attract whatever we want. When the navel chakra is fully open, the world around us will be experienced as our own self that we can model and change at will. If all other chakras are open as well, we will experience our surroundings as paradise.

Closed navel chakra: Despair, sense of being powerless or abuse of power, sense of weakness, lack of willpower, lack of enthusiasm, anger, aggression, frustration, addiction, greed, domination, boredom, sexual problems, inability to change our life for the better, diseases in and around the abdomen and genitals

Root

Location: In the Tibetan Buddhist system the navel and root chakra can be visualised together anywhere between the perineum and the navel – wherever we feel most energy. In the Hindu system the navel chakra is located slightly below the navel and the root chakra sits in our perineum.

Core function: The root chakra indicates how much trust we have in our physical existence and wellbeing and how much we are able to enjoy earthly joys like food and sex. Everything that has been said about the navel chakra is also true for the root chakra.

Open root chakra: Enjoyment of physical pleasures and a feeling of physical security

With kundalini: Same as for the navel chakra

Closed root chakra: Anger, compulsion to argue and fight, sexual problems, survival fears, hypochondria, diseases in and around the abdomen and genitals

Predominance of higher or lower chakras

White Tara taught me that most people suffer from an imbalance of their higher and lower chakras and she also said that it is one of our most important tasks in life to rectify this imbalance. The higher chakras are the heart, throat and head, and the lower chakras are the solar plexus and navel.

If our higher chakras dominate, we approach life with our focus on loving relationships, ideals and the acquisition of knowledge and wisdom. On the negative side, we will lack the power, strength and confidence generated by the lower chakras. This pattern is more often found in women.

If our lower chakras dominate, we approach life with confidence and a strong desire for power and success. On the negative side, we will lack wisdom and compassion for others. This pattern is more often found in men. White Tara explains:

> *The higher chakras are very sensitive, loving and knowing and they help you to feel good in your situation as it is. The lower chakras are tougher and help you to get on in the world and create a better situation. Both sets of chakras need to be balanced perfectly and then you will be happy.*
>
> *Men have a natural tendency to give more through the abdomen - sex, warfare and physical work - and to receive more through the higher chakras. They have a greater need to receive love from a woman because they have less of it themselves. And women receive more through the navel from men because they often do not possess enough power themselves. But all that can change when men and women learn from each other.*
>
> *Your task in life is to keep all chakras blissful simultaneously. Most importantly, you need to combine the power of the lower chakras with the love of the heart and the spiritual understanding of the head by going back and forth between your higher and lower body.*
>
> *If you can narrow the discrepancy between the higher and lower chakras, all the discrepancies in your life will cease. Connecting all chakras in this way is more important than bringing one or two chakras to maximum bliss while neglecting the others.*
>
> *If you are able to shift your main focus from one part of your body to another, it will feel like a second birth. Not everyone gets to experience this second birth – it's a major achievement.*

I was greatly intrigued by these teachings and started to observe in myself and the people around me whether they were true. I found that most people do indeed have a predominance of either higher or lower chakras. While it is true that men in general are more centred in the lower chakras and women are more centred in the higher chakras, it is also possible for both genders to be unbalanced the other way round. Here are some typical examples of how this may look in real life:

Predominance of higher chakras
Imagine a very self-sacrificing woman who works in a caring profession but at home has an alcoholic husband and two out-of-control teenage sons who bully and suppress her.
Imagine a woman who is very spiritual and tries hard do the right and kind thing but in her career feels easily victimised by her more power orientated colleagues.
Imagine a group of ecologically minded people who like to live close to nature but who lack clout and power to assert their point of view in the political arena.
Imagine a very intelligent (nerdy) man who is deeply into his computer world but lacks confidence in dealing with social situations or advancing his career.

Predominance of lower chakras
Imagine a man prone to aggression who bullies others to get his way and who pursues his career egotistically in order to earn money as fast as possible.
Imagine a man who uses spiritual teachings to manipulate others and put himself into a powerful position.
Imagine a gang of aggressive boys who commit random acts of vandalism and criminal acts.
Imagine a woman who uses her good looks and sex appeal to further her career by sleeping with the 'right' men.

Obviously, some of these examples are quite extreme but they make the effects of an imbalance of the higher and lower chakras quite clear. Generally speaking, people with a pre-dominance in the higher chakras lack power while people with a pre-dominance in the lower chakras lack love.

Many people on a spiritual path make the mistake of rejecting the lower chakras as unspiritual in nature. All sexual repression in the name of religion is due to this dynamic. But White Tara encourages us to embrace the lower chakras. This is what she said:

> *There is nothing wrong with earthly joys and if you dismiss them as not sufficiently spiritual, you are simply starving yourself unnecessarily. In people*

> *who have a closed root chakra there is a certain bitterness, which is entirely unnecessary.*

Also, the lower chakras are the seat of the kundalini, whose arousal is a prerequisite to becoming fully enlightened. It is therefore of vital importance to learn to bring the loving qualities of the higher chakras and the powerful qualities of the lower chakras into one harmonious whole. White Tara told me this:

> *In the beginning, you go through the chakras one by one but once you can open them all, it is most important to unite the love and divinity of the upper chakras with the power of the navel. This union will never be quite complete but the gap will become narrower.*

The last sentence is very important because White Tara is making the point that the higher and lower chakras can never be completely united and that there is an inherent discrepancy between power and love that can never be completely overcome. But on our journey to the realisation of our highest potential, we need to do our upmost to bring this inner contradiction into a harmonious whole by becoming more *powerfully loving* or *lovingly powerful*.

If you think about the great beacons of spirituality in human history, you will find that they were able to merge love and power better than the average human being. Both the Buddha and Christ preached the importance of love and at the same time were so powerful that they could inspire billions of people throughout the millennia to follow in their footsteps. Their lives are inspiring examples of just how much good we are able to spread if we can fully unite the power of our lower chakras with the love and wisdom of our higher chakras.

Diagnose the state of your chakras

The first step to improve your chakras is to diagnose the state of your energy system. It might be useful to start a journal of your findings, so that you can observe how your chakras change over time.

Everybody's chakras are open to a certain extent - nobody's chakras are completely closed. How much life force flows within us and how pure this life force is, is a matter of degree. The more open our chakras, the easier and happier our life will become. White Tara explained it to me like this:

The degree of purification in different chakras can vary widely. While some chakras may be open others remain at lower vibrations resulting in all sorts of negative emotions, circumstances, illnesses and difficult relationships. As a result, people feel disjointed in themselves – part of their life works very well, while other parts do not work well at all.

If the heart and head are open but the navel is closed you can experience spiritual ecstasy, insight and love but you will lack the power to attract students to pass it on to. You will also feel easily depleted and the physical world will seem a contradiction to your spiritual bliss. If the throat is also closed, you will be unable to communicate your experiences.

If your head and navel are more open than your heart, you can become very successful but also very ruthless. Your success will feel meaningless. Meaning has always to do with the love of the heart.

In order to diagnose the state of your own chakras you can use the following checklist. Remember that the state of our chakras can change dramatically from minute to minute simply because we may experience strong negative or positive emotions. But we also have a 'base-line' of how open our chakras are on average. Therefore, it is best to choose a time for your chakra diagnosis when you feel reasonably okay.

Exercise: Diagnose your chakras
Ask yourself - which of these three negative emotions you feel most often: anger, sadness or anxiety? Once you have identified the emotion, remember a time when you felt it very strongly and allow the feeling to build. Then check through your body to identify the chakra in which this feeling manifests. Typical places for anger are root/navel and throat chakras; typical places for anxiety are the solar plexus, heart and throat chakras and typical places for sadness are the heart and head chakras. *The chakra you identify as the place where you feel most of your negative emotions is the chakra that you need to heal first!*
Check for locations in your body where you have physical problems and illnesses. *The chakra that is nearest to the painful or sick body part is closed and will need attention at some point. But obviously, also get checked out by a qualified medical practitioner. Chakra work is not a substitute for medical*

> *treatment but will make a good treatment more efficient.*
>
> **Check which areas** of your life throw up continuous problems, for example, love relationships, finances or learning, and use the section 'What each chakra represents' from above to diagnose to which chakras they belong. For example, problems with love relationships belong to the heart chakra, problems with money belong to the navel chakra and problems with learning belong to the head chakra. *At some point you will want to heal the associated chakra, as well.*
>
> **Check whether** you are a person who is predominantly focused on the higher chakras or on the lower chakras by studying the previous section and asking yourself whether you focus more on love or more on power. *If you are more focused on the lower chakras, you need to focus more on love and if you are more focused on the higher chakras you need to focus more on the lower chakras to build up more confidence and power.*
>
> **Now identify** which chakras are working well. Remember a recent time when you were deeply happy and bring to mind the feeling that you felt then. Now check in which chakra this positive emotion manifests. *This is the chakra that is most open in you.*
>
> **Check which areas** of your life work well by using the description of the section 'What each chakra represents'. *Every area that is really satisfying for you is an indication that the associated chakra is working quite well.*
>
> **Write all your findings** in your journal or make a simple drawing of your chakras. The chronic tendencies in our chakras will only improve over time. Therefore, it is best to repeat your chakra diagnosis every few months to see how your energy system is developing.

The sequence of chakra work

Most people have a tendency to maximise one or two chakras in their everyday life while neglecting those that do not work well. Here are two simplified examples: A very intelligent person tends to approach life's challenges solely from the head chakra to the extent that they may end up the proverbial 'nerd'. A very spiritual person may approach life mainly from the heart chakra, which makes them super-sensitive to crude and rude behaviour of others. Both people may also suffer from chronic fatigue or pain due to the missing life force from their navel chakra.

By contrast, someone with a dominant navel chakra may approach life too much from a power perspective and end up in all sorts of power games and without loving relationships. The solution to all these problems is to learn to open *all* chakras evenly, starting with the one that gives us most trouble.

White Tara gave me a very clear road map about the sequence in which we should work with the chakras. From my own experience and also from the experiences with my clients, I have found White Tara's advice very useful. She says:

> *The most important chakra for achieving overall happiness is the heart chakra. If you want to change your situation, you always need to change the heart first and foremost through the practice of loving-kindness and devotion to your deity.*

As you know, I have empathised many times that we always need to practice loving-kindness alongside any other practice. The reason for this is the importance of the heart chakra. Without an open heart chakra no other spiritual practice makes sense because love is the final goal of all our spiritual endeavours. White Tara continues:

> *Then you work on the chakra that presents the greatest problems for you in an emotional sense. Emotions are more important than physical symptoms. Your deepest issues will appear as psychosomatic diseases. They are like the hardened crust at the bottom of the chakra. They can be dealt with after you have dealt with your emotional issues.*

> *The last chakra you should work on is the navel, because its strong energy would otherwise throw up too many unresolved issues from the higher chakras. But once all the other chakras are open, it will energise them and will make them even more blissful and powerful.*

> *If you are centred too much in the higher chakras then focusing on the crown will greatly exacerbate that imbalance. The same happens if you are centred too much in the lower chakras and then focus on the navel or root chakras. That is why it is wise to leave the crown and the navel chakra in peace as long as you are less developed.*

Once all our chakras are open, it is important to find the overall balance between the upper and lower chakras that we have talked about in the previous sections. White Tara explains:

Once all chakras are opened, your main goal should be to unite the upper chakras and the lower chakras into a more harmonious whole. You do this by moving between the higher and the lower chakras so that you focus evenly on both sets.

By learning to respond to life equally from the higher and lower sets of chakras we become more whole and complete. It is important to understand that this will be an on-going process, just like the ability to balance a scale or ride a bike requires on-going attention. Once we are finally able to keep this balance intact, we will be rewarded with a life that is equally loving, wise and powerful.

The following case study is fictitious and is loosely based on my own life. It is meant to illustrate the sequence involved in working with the chakras in the way that White Tara has outlined here for us. (My real life was much more convoluted than this case study suggests.)

> **Case study: Janet, 54 years (fictitious)**
> Janet started to meditate at the age of 24 and was first introduced to loving-kindness meditation. She practised this meditation for five years and it helped her to align herself deeply with spiritual values and to become a much kinder person than she had been before. As a result, long-term feelings of loneliness disappeared. Janet was able to let go of the resentment she harboured against her parents' neglectful parenting and she met and married her husband with whom she has now a deeply happy marriage.
>
> Despite her happy marriage, Janet suffered occasionally from depression and learnt that by focusing on her forehead chakra these feelings went away. The forehead chakra practice also stimulated her creativity and insight and she started to write poetry and paint Buddhist tankhas.
>
> The next chakra Janet focused on was her throat chakra because she felt shy and lacked confidence in social situations. The throat chakra practice was very effective and Janet became confident enough to speak her mind and start her own counselling practice.
>
> The subsequent chakra that presented problems for Janet was her solar plexus chakra because she often suffered from stomach pain and found it hard to relax deeply. Once she had worked with the stomach chakra her tensions and also her stomach pain went away and she felt a deep sense of peace.
>
> Finally, Janet was ready for her kundalini awakening and focused for a long

> time on her navel chakra. As a result, she experienced most of the symptoms and benefits described in the first two chapters of this book.

Summary of the sequence of chakra work
Firstly, work with the heart chakra
Secondly, work on the forehead, throat or solar plexus chakra starting with the chakra where you feel most negative emotions (but not yet on crown and navel/root chakra)
Thirdly, work with the navel/root chakra in order to awaken the kundalini
Fourthly, carry on attending to the chakra that throws up most negative emotions and pain
Fifthly, balance the upper and lower chakras

How to open a chakra
There are five main approaches to opening a chakra and ideally they would all be used more or less simultaneously. In practice, however, we are best off consciously practicing them one by one and then focusing mostly on the approach that works best for us. Be aware, however, that sometimes a chakra can throw up deep-seated resistance. It is then advisable to return to all the other approaches and see what works. The five approaches to open a chakra are:

Love
Relaxation
Devotion to a deity
Using images, sounds or a memory as a trigger
Observation rather than doing

We should begin all chakra practices by imagining our entire body as hollow and filled with radiant light. The brighter the light in our inner vision, the easier our chakra work will be. Do not be too specific about the exact location of a particular chakra but focus roughly in the middle of entire body regions, like the chest, head or lower abdomen.

Opening a chakra through love
The first step for any form of self-development work should always be self-love because under the influence of love everything becomes pliable and soft. By

contrast, a pushy or even aggressive approach will make everything hard and resistant. We have already discussed the importance of self-love in chapter three and we should always start our chakra and kundalini work by loving ourselves with all of our problems and imperfections.

Opening a chakra through love is not difficult. You simply smile lovingly towards the chakra that you wish to open, just like a mother smiles at her beloved child. It is particularly important to maintain this loving attitude if you detect some blockage in the form of numbness, pain or negative feelings in the chakra you want to open. Visualise this love as a beautiful light and lovingly and tenderly caress and penetrate your chakra with your light, including any pain and negative emotions.

After doing this for some time (this could be minutes or weeks) you will feel a softening in the chakra and eventually a beautiful blissful feeling in this body region. This bliss is a sign that your chakra is opening. After this first opening it is important to recall this bliss frequently until it becomes more stable.

Opening a chakra through relaxation

Remember that every chakra consists of the sea of love and the life force. If the life force is tense and distorted, our chakra is blocked. Through relaxing deeply we can access the sea of love and once we are more in touch with the sea of love, it will be easier to tune into the divine vibration of the life force. White Tara says succinctly:

> *The most important thing to open a chakra is relaxation – very deep relaxation.*

In the work with my clients, I have found that a very good way to relax a chakra is by imagining a flower bud that opens out from the chakra. Virtually all my clients feel that this image is helpful. This is how it works:

Exercise: Open a chakra with the image of an opening flower bud
Start by imagining your body as hollow and filled with brilliant light.
Know that the numbness, negative emotion or pain in your chakra is a form of tension and imagine this tension as a tight flower bud.
With the out-breath imagine opening the flower bud and release all tensions in that body part. Imagine beautiful coloured light emerging from the open flower and radiating to the end of the universe in small undulating waves. Follow the beautiful light in your mind.

> *At the end of the out-breath* do not inhale immediately but have a break that is as long as possible. Carry on following the light from your open flower radiating further and further away. At the same time deeply relax your entire body.
> *Before you feel* uncomfortable, breathe in again.
> *On the out-breath* see the flower bud opening again and the light flowing out once more. Repeat for several minutes.

Another way to relax the area of a chakra is through stretching and massage. You do not need to be a yoga expert to stretch – simply bend forward, backward and sideways in the area of your chakra. Do these stretches slowly and with great awareness. Pause after each stretch and feel into the chakra to notice the effects. In a similar way, gently or vigorously rub, knead or knock the body area around a chakra for a few seconds and then pause to notice the effects of the massage. I have also found a small handheld electrical massager to be helpful in relaxing the area of a chakra. Consciously relax the chakra when stretching and massaging yourself.

Open a chakra through devotion to a deity

White Tara always made a strong point to me that devotion to a divine being is crucial if we are to open our chakras and indeed develop spiritually at all. She probably focused on this point so strongly because I have a history of a misguided search for too much independence.

As a younger person, I used to believe that given the right technique I could simply enlighten myself. I know I am not alone in this faulty attitude because I have met many meditation students who also have problems with the devotional aspect of spiritual development. However, White Tara explained to me that the essence of every spiritual progress is love. And love means to literally unite with someone else – with someone who is further on the path than we are. Only through this union, White Tara insisted, can we be introduced to a higher vibration that was unknown to us before. Accepting and integrating the higher vibration of our higher power into our own being is what we call the process of opening our chakras. In order to achieve this, we need to surrender to a higher being with love and devotion. Here are White Tara's words:

> *You cannot open your chakras solely by yourself. Opening your chakras happens first and foremost through loving relationships. The highest energy*

> *comes of course from the deity and if you are able, you should focus on her first and foremost.*

For some people, surrendering to a divine being comes easily and they do not need to be shown how to do this. They are the gifted students and they are rare. For the rest of us, White Tara gives us this technique:

> *Once your chakra is deeply relaxed, you need to let yourself be affected in your chakra by divine vibrations. You may imagine 'sucking in' energy from a deity. However, in reality you do not suck anything in. You are simply tuning in to the higher vibrations of the deity.*

The traditional technique in Tibetan Buddhism is to imagine your deity in front of you and see a beam of light emerging from one of their chakras and then entering into the corresponding chakra of your own: a white beam for the head, red for the throat, blue for the heart, yellow for the solar plexus and green for the navel.

In my own practice and through teaching my students, I have found that we do not need to follow these instructions rigidly and that it can often be easier to adapt the colours and images to our own needs, as long as we get the essence of the meditation right. And the essence is the love and devotion we feel towards the deity. It is also important always to imagine brilliant light and not dull and dark colours.

Exercise: Opening a chakra through devotion to your deity

Imagine your body as hollow and filled with brilliant light and imagine your deity surrounded by beautiful light in front of you. Use any of the following imagery, whichever works best:

Imagine white light coming from one of the chakras of your deity and entering into your corresponding chakra.

Imagine the deity right in front of your body with their chakras touching your chakras. Imagine each pair of chakras merging together.

Imagine the entire deity entering into your chakra like milk flowing into water.

Imagine small deities flying into your chakra.

Imagine a small deity sitting within one of your own chakras radiating with light.

Using images, sounds or memories as a trigger to open a chakra

Another way of opening a chakra is repeating a word or visualising an image associated with that chakra. In Tibetan Buddhism and also in Hinduism there are traditional mantra sounds and visualisations that are associated with each chakra, for example, 'om' for the head, 'ah' for the throat and 'hum' for the heart. However, in my experience it can be more useful to find your own words and images that speak more directly to you.

If, for example, you have a Christian leaning, then an image of Christ or Our Lady may guide you more quickly into a divine vibration than visualising complicated Sanskrit syllables or Tibetan Buddhist deities that you have not previously heard about.

I have also found that using words that carry meaning for you is more effective in opening a chakra, rather than foreign syllables that do not affect you on a deeper level. For example, associating the word 'bliss' with the head chakra or the word 'love' with the heart chakra may be much more effective than reciting the syllables 'om' and 'hum', which may carry more meaning for people who are rooted in a Buddhist culture.

When saying a word like 'love' or 'joy' it is important to evoke the associated feeling in your body-mind and not repeat these words in a mechanical way. So, for example, the word love should evoke a loving feeling in your chest and the word peace should evoke a peaceful feeling in your stomach area. Do not be discouraged if on some days your chakras feel quite numb. It takes time and persistence to stabilise a blissful vibration in a chakra that you can call on at will.

Another approach is remembering a happy memory that is connected to a positive feeling in a particular chakra. For example, in order to open the heart chakra you can try to remember a moment when you felt deep love. Or in order to open the throat chakra, you can remember a time when you laughed a lot with a good friend or spoke very confidently.

It is easy to work with these words or memories in daily life and to evoke the feeling associated with the chakra simply by repeating the words and images from time to time - but remember never to do this mechanically. Eventually, simply remembering a certain word, image or memory will help you to open your chakra and tune into the right vibration. You will know if a chakra is open by the feeling of wellbeing and even bliss you can experience in this part of your body.

Here is a selection of words and images that my students or myself have used with good effect. But you can also make up your own images and words. Play around with words, mantras or images until you have found those that really work for you. And do not forget to visualise your body as hollow and filled with brilliant light while experimenting.

Head
Images: *Your higher power, a white light, an angelic being*
Words: *Bliss, joy, peace*
Memories: *Remember a very happy moment (chances are that this memory is associated with your head chakra)*

Throat
Images: *Laughing friends, a beautiful light, a colourful flower*
Words: *Joy, confidence, laughter*
Memories: *Remember a time when you were very happy and confident, able to laugh and communicate freely*

Heart
Images: *A hugging couple, a new-born baby, comforting a little anxious child, your higher power, a beautiful light*
Words: *Love, caring, compassion, kindness*
Memories: *Remember a moment when you deeply loved someone, maybe a newborn baby, a pet or a child*

Solar Plexus
Images: *A still lake, a flower meadow, an open blue sky with drifting clouds*
Words: *Peace, stillness*
Memories: *Remember a time when you were able to be deeply peaceful and tranquil in a beautiful spot in nature*

Observing instead of doing
Once you start noting any positive feelings in a chakra, it is paramount to simply observe rather than trying to make the feeling bigger and better. The joy and bliss in your body and mind are your true nature, so there is no need to manipulate them in any way. What we are trying to achieve here is to 'tune into' a certain vibration and not to manufacture or fabricate it. The more often we simply tune into the wonderful feeling that is already there, the easier it will become to do it

more frequently and finally to stabilise it.

So, as soon you can feel a gentle sense of wellbeing in a chakra, stop all further effort and simply focus on this feeling to the exclusion of all other thoughts and images. See this blissful feeling as a beautiful light and you will notice how it expands and grows on its own accord. Simply observe this process and relax. If your mind wanders, simply come back to the trigger that opened your chakra until you sense the feeling of wellbeing and bliss once again. Then start observing this feeling in a relaxed way and repeat this process over and over.

The complete practice of chakra opening
Preparation

Resolve to do this chakra meditation not only for yourself but also for the best of all beings.

Imagine your higher power in front of you filled and surrounded by beautiful light. Your higher power is smiling at you with deepest love and wishes for you to be happy and enlightened.

Tune in to the love of your higher power and love yourself including all your weaknesses and imperfections.

Visualise your body as hollow and filled with brilliant light.

Opening a chakra

Notice the warm and pleasant feeling that arises as a result of your preparation. Notice in which chakra or body part it manifests primarily. See this feeling as a beautiful light and focus on this sense of wellbeing and light without trying to make it stronger or better. Notice how it expands on its own accord.

Alternatively, recall a happy memory. Once you can feel a sense of happiness let the memory gently fall away and simply observe the feeling. Notice in which chakra or body part it manifests primarily. See this feeling as a beautiful light and focus on this sense of wellbeing and light without trying to make it stronger or better. Notice how it expands of its own accord.

The chakra in which this positive feeling manifests is your best-developed chakra. Focus on the entire body region around this chakra rather than just a small point.

Work with this chakra using one or all of the following approaches as explained in the previous sections:

Smile into the chakra with love.

Deeply relax the chakra through imagining a flower opening.
Merge that chakra with your higher power.
Associate the chakra with a word, image or memory, so that it will be easier to remember the positive feeling.
Focus on the wellbeing and beautiful light in this chakra until it becomes stronger and stronger and all-encompassing. Refrain from trying to manipulate this feeling in any way. Simply observe.
If you experience any distracting thoughts and feelings, simply let them go, relax and come back to your chakra work over and over again.

Opening more chakras

Your next chakra should be the heart chakra if you have not already worked with it.
If you have already worked with the heart, next choose the chakra that throws up most negative emotions. In order to find that chakra, remember how you feel when you are angry, upset or depressed and notice in which body part this feeling manifests. This is the chakra you want to work with next.
Go back to the good feeling from the chakra that you found easy to open. Sometimes the positive feeling from your 'easy' chakra will simply enlarge into another chakra.
Work with your second chakra as described in the previous sections. ***Use*** one or all of the following approaches, whatever works best:
Smile into the chakra with love.
Deeply relax the chakra through imagining a flower opening.
Merge that chakra with your higher power.
Associate the chakra with a word, image or memory, so that it will be easier to remember the positive feeling.
Focus on the wellbeing and beautiful light in this chakra until it becomes stronger and stronger and all encompassing. Refrain from trying to manipulate this feeling in any way. Simply observe.
If you find it hard to let go of negative feelings send love to yourself or anybody who is involved in your negative feeling until you feel better.
If you feel numbness or physical tensions in a chakra you can try to stretch your physical body in this place by gently bending backward, sideways or forward. Or you can try to massage this chakra with your hands or massager. Do the stretches or the massage in a gentle way and focus with awareness on all the

> feelings this evokes.
> ***If you experience*** any distracting thoughts and feelings, simply let them go and come back to your chakra work over and over.
>
> ***Ending the meditation***
> ***End*** your meditation by dedicating all its benefits to the best of all beings.

More advice on opening your chakras

In the following paragraphs I will go over the most important aspects of opening your chakras so that you can, hopefully, avoid the various pitfalls that may lie ahead.

The importance of being patient and taking your time

Take ample time to work through the chakra opening meditation. Only proceed to the next step once you can fully experience the earlier parts. It may take numerous sessions until you can go through the entire chakra meditation in one sitting and that is okay. Chakra meditation is a long-term process and trying to rush it will be counter-productive.

Depending on the amount of disturbances in each chakra, you may have to spend several months with each chakra before it is finally completely open. During this time, you should also lightly work with all the other the chakras (apart from the crown and the navel), in order to avoid imbalances in your chakra system. But the main focus of your daily practice should be the chakra that throws up most emotional problems.

If the notion of having to work for several months with each chakra appears too much for you, remember that working with the chakras already awakens the kundalini in a mild and controlled way. If you are wise, you will not hurry this process along. Always keep the many changes that I have described in the second chapter in mind. You will need time to accommodate and integrate all these changes. When it comes to a kundalini awakening, 'slower is faster'.

The importance of focusing on your chakras all day long

Ideally, you should be focusing all day long on the chakra that you would like to open. Obviously, this cannot be achieved second by second but the more often you can come back to the chakra you want to open, the sooner you will be successful. In order to achieve this you can install inconspicuous reminders in your life like little self-adhesive dots around your house and car or you could carry a mala (a string of beads). Anything that will remind you to focus your mind over and over again on your chakra will be helpful.

The importance of devotion to your higher power
Remember that White Tara always emphasised the importance of deep devotion to your higher power. Chakra opening is not a mechanical process but a tuning into a higher vibration. This higher vibration comes from your higher power or your spiritual teacher. It is important to avoid thinking that you can somehow enlighten yourself, which would be strengthening your ego rather than diminishing it.

The importance of visualising beautiful light
When working with our energy system the power of visualisation is very important. As I have already described, you need to visualise your body as hollow and filled with beautiful light. When you send love to yourself and others, visualise this love as a layer of radiant light that you gently wrap around yourself and other people. You should also use this light to penetrate all the 'blocks' in your chakras. Once you feel a sense of wellbeing in a chakra, visualise this feeling as a beautiful light, as well. Just be careful not to manipulate these feelings or to try making them bigger or better. Just learn to 'see' these positive feelings as a beautiful light.

Some people believe that they cannot visualise but luckily that is not true. Everybody can visualise and everybody does it all the time. Simply being able to find your way around your hometown depends on your ability to visualise. I think people assume that visualising means to see things as clearly as if they were real. But that level of clarity is not necessary. Visualising beautiful light can be as basic as having a vague sense of this light. As you regularly practice, your ability to see things in your mind will rapidly improve.

The importance of witness consciousness
While working with the chakras you may experience all sorts of weird and wonderful body sensations. Remember always to 'witness' these appearances as you have learnt in chapter three and not to identify with them. Otherwise there is a danger of trying to push negative feelings away and being attached to positive feelings. This aversion and attachment will interfere with the process of opening your chakras and getting in touch with your divine nature.

Once you have a gentle feeling of happiness, it is especially important to simply witness it and not to try to make it stronger or better. Just focusing on this feeling is enough to allow it expand on its own accord.

The importance of seeing 'blocks' in the chakras as psychological in nature

The spiritual literature of Buddhism and Hinduism sometimes appears mechanical in its description of the chakras and energy channels. But we should not see our energy system as something like an elaborate plumbing system. On the contrary, when we experience a 'block' in a chakra we need to keep in mind that we are not dealing with anything material. Chakras are 'blocked' for one reason alone and that is our fear, anger and hopelessness and the faulty beliefs that led to these negative emotions.

For example, if we are afraid of not having enough love in our life, we will tense up around our heart and these tensions will result in a blocked heart chakra. If we believe that wielding any form of power will make us a bad person, we are blocking our navel chakra and if someone denies the existence of the divine, their head chakra is blocked even if they are very intelligent.

It is not always necessary to find the exact negative belief that led to our blocked chakra but it is necessary to investigate the general 'topic' of a chakra, particularly if it remains blocked for a longer period of time. After we have identified the problem, we need to do whatever we can to improve that area of our life. By contrast, if we believe that our chakra blocks are purely mechanical 'energy phenomena', we will, in fact, cement them into place. Our materialistic outlook is one of the reasons that our chakra became blocked in the first place.

The importance of avoiding the crown and navel chakra

Do not work intensively with the crown or navel chakras until the forehead, throat, heart and solar plexus chakras are all open. The navel chakra will awaken the kundalini and if this happens prematurely, you will experience the impurities in the higher chakras much more strongly, which can be uncomfortable.

When working with the head chakra, always focus on the forehead and not on the top of the head (crown chakra in the Hindu system) as the focus on the crown can bring up premature kundalini awakening and uncomfortable side effects.

The importance of not getting attached to the bliss

Once we get more bliss in the chakras, we may experience a frustrating dynamic: after spells of intense bliss there is a sense of comedown just like a comedown after a particularly wonderful drug trip. This can be frustrating and confusing, especially if we are not prepared and have not been warned about this dynamic.

It is important not to expect that your bliss will last forever. On the contrary, you should be warned that your ordinary life may sometimes appear as even more boring and frustrating in comparison to your wonderful meditation. This dynamic will become even more pronounced once your kundalini gives you extremely intense spells of ecstasy. When the intensity of this bliss clashes with your ordinary reality, it can be real test of your spiritual maturity.

Spiritual maturity means to always remember that the actual point of all our spiritual exercises is to become a more loving person who can contribute to the wellbeing of others. The purpose of experiencing bliss in our meditation is not to have a good time (even though it will be an extremely good time!) but to enable us to love and help others more and to understand more about our true nature.

The remedy for getting too attached to the bliss is to have a strong resolution to value love more than bliss. In practical terms, that means that whenever other people's problems or weaknesses are disturbing our bliss, we should be prepared to give up our wonderful experience and attend to their needs. Failing to do so is the main danger on the path of kundalini and will actually delay or even reverse our spiritual development.

I myself have experienced the shocking rushes of anger that seemed to appear out of nowhere when the needs of my husband and son disrupted my wonderful bliss experiences. Luckily, I was aware of why that was happening and did not allow myself to give in to these negative tendencies. But I will tell you that this is not always easy because our anger usually seems to be totally justified. It is for that reason that we must never forget to practice love and kindness meditation alongside our kundalini practice.

The importance of noticing the first moments of non-self

When you experience stronger feelings of happiness and bliss, notice how your usual sense of identity fades during these experiences. Everything that you took to be your usual sense of self - your background, your character and how your past has shaped you – starts losing its significance. Instead, you can see and feel that the bliss in each chakra is an experience of open space and actually expands into infinity without core or boundary. Notice this and know that this is the beginning of an experience of your true self – your divine essence.

It is important not to develop any idea that you 'own' the bliss or your divine essence and to know that these experiences do not make you into some sort of superior being. Instead, focus on the spacious experience of the bliss in which any idea of having a self is fading. Failing to recognise this sense of non-self could lead to ego-inflation, which is the opposite of what we want to achieve on our spiritual path.

Possible problems when opening a chakra

Many problems with opening the chakras result from thinking about the process in a too mechanistic way. Chakras are not really flower buds that we 'open', even though it is useful to visualise them that way. If we experience problems with opening our chakras, we need to remember what chakras really are: they are a combination of our life force and the sea of love. So, when we talk about 'opening' a chakra, it means coming back to the perfect balance of the sea of love and the life force, which feels like open loving acceptance and bliss.

As we have learnt in chapter one, all suffering originates from a disharmony of the sea of love and our life force, resulting in the life force getting distorted into the experience of negative emotions. In other words, a lack of love changes the vibration of a chakra from bliss to a tight, tense and disharmonious vibration, which appears as fear, anger, greed or depression.

In order to remedy this situation, we need to focus on our chakras with deep love and acceptance and we need to include all our weaknesses and imperfections in this love, as well as forgive everyone who has ever hurt us. In the light of this all-encompassing and forgiving love, everything becomes pliable and 'willing' to change. The distorted vibration of the life force in the form of our negative emotions will then return to its virgin state, which is pure, open and blissful.

On the other hand, if we approach chakra opening with an impatient 'doer' attitude, we are likely to get stuck and experience many blockages. The key is love, relaxation and surrender to our higher consciousness. The enemies in this process are impatience, competitiveness and negative pre-conceived ideas about others and ourselves.

The general advice for all these problems is not to try too hard because this impatient pressure creates exactly the knots and tightness that we want to let go. Therefore, if you find yourself getting frustrated, simply limit your meditation to the preparatory practices of witness consciousness, loving-kindness and devotion to your higher consciousness for a while. You can do this for anything between a few minutes and up to several weeks and then focus again on the chakras.

What follows are typical problems you may encounter when opening the chakras and what you can do about them.

If you cannot get to the feeling of wellbeing
If you cannot feel the feeling of wellbeing in a chakra, my advice is to simply go back to witness consciousness and loving kindness for a few days or even weeks. Focus particularly on loving yourself and accepting yourself just as you are with all your weaknesses and shortcomings and forgiving everyone who has hurt you. It is also important to strengthen your relationship with your higher power through devotional practices and prayer.

You may simply need more time and it is important not to get impatient. Impatience is a subtle form of anger and it may be this anger that is blocking the opening of your chakras.

If you are suffering from depression or other strong negative emotions which do not go away after practicing loving-kindness and witness consciousness, I recommend you work with higher-consciousness healing, as described in my book The Five-Minute Miracle, or find a suitable psychotherapist to help you.

If you cannot feel anything and your chakras seem numb
The most important factor in being able to feel something in a chakra is relaxation. Imagine that your chakra is a frozen piece of ice and that relaxing the area of your body is like melting the ice.

Use whatever method may help you to relax more deeply. You can think of different images like a drop of water falling into the chakra as if into a lake and ripples of energy waves extending from the centre into infinity. You could also imagine the chakra as a piece of ice melting in the sun. Use these images while giving yourself a gentle massage or stretching your body in this place.

If you still have trouble feeling anything, you may be one of those people who suppress their emotions. This suppression may be the result of an emotionally repressed upbringing but it may also result from a spiritual misunderstanding. Some meditation practitioners believe that spiritual people should always be calm and serene and they try hard to appear that way even though in reality they are merely repressing their emotions.

As you can imagine, this approach is counter-productive and pushes people even more deeply into their ego-defences rather than liberating them. The path of kundalini is the path of energy and this energy is felt foremost as emotions in our mind-stream. We cannot be totally serene, emotionless and have a kundalini awakening at the same time. We need to allow ourselves to feel our feelings. It is important to understand that feeling our emotions does not necessarily imply acting on them.

In order to rectify a possible repressive tendency, try focusing more on your feelings than your thoughts and body sensations. You should do that in daily life and particularly during your practice of witness consciousness and loving-kindness.

You may also be one of those people who stop themselves from feeling enthusiastic and happy by saying things to yourself like, 'don't get over-excited, you will just be disappointed later on.' Instead, allow yourself to feel the fear that is behind this ego-defence. With awareness comes choice and hopefully you will become able to allow yourself more joy and happiness.

Another approach to getting more in touch with your emotions is to notice how you shield yourself from feeling upset the next time an opportunity arises. Instead of using your usual defence mechanism, let yourself be affected by your emotions and by the pain of others. It may not be pleasant to actually feel these emotions but by allowing yourself to experience negative feelings you will also enable yourself to experience positive feelings. Eventually, you will be able to feel the bliss of your true nature.

It also helps if you can express your emotions in an exaggerated, funny way - like a clown in a circus. Simply, allow yourself to be silly and to act melodramatically. If you find it hard to act like a clown, you may be taking yourself too seriously. Do whatever it takes to lighten up and develop some healthy self-deprecating humour.

If you are engulfed in negative emotions

If you feel engulfed in feelings of strong anger, tears or anxiety, you may have already more kundalini flowing than you can deal with. In which case, you need to back off and focus more on witness consciousness and loving-kindness until these emotions subside.

I also recommend the approach of higher-consciousness healing that I have described in my book The Five-Minute Miracle, which reveals an excellent method for overcoming negative emotions.

If these two recommendations do not work for you, you may need to work with a therapist in order to sort out the underlying conflicts in your life that have led to all these negative emotions.

If you cannot concentrate
Lack of focus is a common problem that is often made worse by our current culture of round-the-clock entertainment. I recommend that you dramatically curtail your use of computer, television and phone for entertainment purposes and allow yourself to feel a bit of boredom.

Once you have a little more time, use it for meditation. If you still find it hard to concentrate, use a concentration aid like counting your breaths, saying mantras or using a mala to count beads. Don't expect that this approach will feel particularly pleasant because lack of focus is an ego-defence that serves the purpose of warding off uncomfortable feelings, most of all anger.

If you manage to become more focused, you are also likely to feel more frustration and anger and that is of course disturbing, initially. But if this happens, you should congratulate yourself that you have improved your ability to concentrate, and then work with loving-kindness to dissolve the anger.

If you get 'weird' energy experiences
If you get weird energy experiences like a feeling of tingling, buzzing, churning, jerking or sensations of heat, cold or of animals moving in your body, you can see all this as a sign that your kundalini has started to awaken.

First of all, do not be afraid. While these energy experiences can certainly be weird and sometimes also uncomfortable, they are not dangerous. I have yet to see someone who has been harmed or damaged by 'weird' energy experiences. In other words, feeling strong energies in your head or chest is no more dangerous than feeling strong sexual energies in your lower abdomen when you are sexually aroused.

Most problems that I see in my kundalini clients are created through their *resistance* towards the kundalini energy – not through the kundalini itself. It is the fear of the kundalini energy and aversion towards it that creates the problems and may even drive people to believe that they are going mad. The more fearful and averse they are, the more it will hurt. As soon as people know and trust that kundalini is essentially a positive force, most problems subside and become manageable.

I will say more about kundalini problems in the chapter six. For now, I simply advise you to relax, to observe and to say to yourself, 'even if it feels very real, it is all just in my mind. There is nothing to be afraid of.'

If you feel physical pain in the chakra

If you feel physical tensions or pain in a chakra, first rule out any diseases by going to a doctor. If you are sure that there is nothing physically wrong with your body, remember to visualise your body as hollow and filled with brilliant light. Then try to massage the area of your chakra or stretch it and work with this chakra as explained in the chakra exercise. Remember to relax deeply and not be afraid.

If the pain persists, you may be suffering from energy overload. The remedy for this problem is to stop giving this chakra any further attention. I will say more about dealing with this energy overload in chapter six.

Chapter five
Awakening the Kundalini

My own story

After my initial kundalini awakening at the age of 24, I experienced the deep crisis I described in chapter one. This was exacerbated by the many pre-existing psychological problems I had before my first kundalini awakening. I was born into a family of two alcoholic parents and experienced abuse and rejection as a child and teenager. As a result, I suffered from many fears, as well as loneliness and depression.

But once I entered a Tibetan Buddhist centre a year after my first kundalini awakening, I just knew that I had been 'rescued' and that I had come home. I deeply engrossed myself in my new community and spent many evenings each week sitting at the feet of Buddhist teachers in order to learn about the spiritual concepts that were so new and exciting to me. It really was one of those 'born-again' transformations given that only one year earlier I had been a rather hard-line atheist.

A year later, I went to a little known German Buddhist teacher who was in the process of developing a small Buddhist community in the south of France. This teacher worked with us using unorthodox methods, freely mixing Eastern meditative approaches with Western radical forms of psychotherapy. With hindsight, I can now clearly see that this teacher had awakened kundalini, too. At the time, Gopi Krishna's book about kundalini had just come out and our teacher discussed this book with us in detail. However, I did not recognise myself in Gopi Krishna's descriptions which were far more extreme than what I had gone through.

During my three years with this Buddhist group, I was introduced to a wide array of practices for personal and spiritual growth. I was greatly interested in all of this and used these practices to heal and resolve my many personal problems. At some point my teacher trained with Mantak Chia who taught energy and kundalini practices from a Taoist point of view. We all practiced diligently and this deepened and calmed my own kundalini process and benefitted me greatly.

A lot of what was happening in this group could be described as some sort of 'laughter therapy'. My teacher thought that we were all much too serious and repressed and that laughter was the best way to undo our ego-defences. So when one of us had a problem, he made us take a guitar and sing a tragic-comic song while the rest of the group dissolved into laughter. We had so much fun! I remember numerous occasions when we were literally writhing around on the floor squealing and screeching in fits of almost hysterical laughter as we played out our neuroses and relationship problems in funny ways.

Obviously, a lot of our problems were centred on sexual relationships and by bringing so much laughter and joy into this topic we liberated our sexuality. At the same time, it made my kundalini rise more strongly.

Unfortunately, there was a dark side to this group too and sometimes this 'laughter therapy' descended into some sort of public humiliation. There were also a number of students who became too entangled with our teacher because they conducted business together, built several houses in the South of France and at the same time tried to be in a devoted spiritual teacher-student relationship. It was all too much and, after some time, people became more and more resentful. So, after three very adventurous and deeply transformative years, this group came to an end.

While many of my fellow students left the group with long-lasting resentments, I emerged from it at the age of 29 greatly transformed and healed from many of the psychological wounds of my upbringing. Through all that laughing and singing my throat chakra had opened and the debilitating social fear I had experienced in my throat since I had been a teenager had vanished. As a result I became confident enough to start my training as a psychotherapist, which I found hugely fulfilling. Also, the emphasis on liberating our sexuality had opened my abdominal chakra and, from then on, my ability to connect to a man on a sexual level became a source of happiness instead of a source of frustration as it had been before.

In the following years, I felt much happier within myself but I still felt that I was strangely different from 'normal society' and that 'something' was driving me on to immerse myself more and more deeply into my personal development and spiritual practices. I had many strange energy and paranormal experiences, which I discussed with a few Buddhist friends who had had similar experiences. With hindsight, I can now clearly see that some of these Buddhist friends also had awakened kundalini without knowing it.

I still struggled with loneliness and depressive feelings at times but I worked very hard to overcome these problems with any technique of spiritual and personal growth that I came across. In time I learnt to accept myself more fully and made peace with my feeling of being so different from normal society. I trained in various forms of psychotherapy and started to work as a counsellor and a few years later also as meditation teacher, and found all that very fulfilling.

My spiritual teacher during my early thirties was Rigdzin Shikpo, a student of the famous Tibetan Buddhist lama Chögyam Trungpa Rinpoche, and my main spiritual practice in these years was loving-kindness. Through this practice my kundalini became much calmer and my heart chakra opened, which brought many positive improvements to my life. For the first time in my adult life I did not feel lonely anymore, my friendships became more loving and mutually supportive and I felt more inner happiness than ever before. I even had occasional experiences of intense bliss and started to become more clairvoyant. However, I still did not have a clue that all these positive developments were caused by my kundalini awakening from ten years earlier.

From Rigdzin Shikpo I learnt wish-practice, which is the Buddhist term for the more commonly known techniques around manifesting your dreams. Once I had learnt how to use these, I threw myself into it and, due to my awakened kundalini, became quite successful at it. Between the age of 36 and 40 I met and married my wonderful husband, moved to England, started to work as a self-employed psychotherapist and meditation teacher, developed higher-consciousness healing – a psychotherapeutic method that proved to be extraordinarily effective, had a baby and had three books published - despite not speaking English very well.

All these things I had manifested by using Buddhist wish-practice. I believed in these techniques but it also shocked me how powerful they were. For example, after I had been with my husband-to-be for a few months he bought a house for us that looked exactly like the one I had been visualising for four years in great detail. I had vividly visualised this white house by a lake while believing it was impossible to actually live in such a house because in Germany, where I lived at the time, houses are never built by lakes. Also, most Germans live in flats and only the rich can afford a whole house. So I had 'known' that owning a house by a lake was out of the question for me and I had only visualised it as a sort of backdrop for my 'perfect relationship and work'. What I did not know was that my future husband was English and that in England it was quite possible to buy an affordable house near a lake!

These were truly transformative years that left my friends and family bewildered and also a bit envious, as I had been on a trajectory of under-achievement, poverty and loneliness. In hindsight, I see my ability to manifest a life that was so much improved as a direct result of my awakened kundalini. If you are interested in these practices, please have a look at my book Advanced Manifesting in which I describe this technique in great detail.

The next fresh influx of kundalini energy happened to me at the age of 39 when I first heard of the Tibetan Buddhist teacher Garchen Rinpoche from a friend. Before I even met this lama I prayed to him in meditation and 'heard' him say, 'just be happy'. And that was that, 'just be happy'.

What followed can only be described as an ascent into ecstasy. The kundalini energy rose to my head chakra and from that moment onwards the sun was always shining in my life like a freely flowing source of joy and happiness that never stopped, even when something negative happened. Before this development I had depended – just like everybody else – on good things happening in order to be happy. This changed dramatically from then on as my need for things and people to make me happy dramatically reduced, while the source of joy and happiness in my brain spouted endless happy feelings.

I was of course thrilled with this development and thought that I had finally understood 'everything' about Buddhism and enlightenment. But obviously, it wasn't quite that easy and there were more challenges to come. Like many of my own kundalini clients, I went through a prolonged phase of intense anxiety, which came from using some Ayurveda medicine that was considered 'totally safe'. What I did not know was that even these safe alternative approaches to medicine can produce massive side effects for someone in a kundalini process. But I still did not know that this was 'my problem'.

The anxiety was severe and was sometimes accompanied by mild hallucinations but it also felt somewhat unreal because I was also experiencing all this bliss at the same time. Nevertheless, it went on for nearly two years and I had to work very hard to overcome it. The result was that I developed the anti-anxiety technique that I will share with you in chapter six.

Once the anxiety was gone, I asked Garchen Rinpoche for the tummo initiation (Tibetan equivalent for kundalini) at the age of 42. He willingly explained to me how to do this and I started to practice diligently with the breathing exercises he had shown me. Unfortunately, my old depressive feelings came back and I could not continue to practice in that way. So I started to read extensively about kundalini to find out why I could not practice the tummo exercise without getting depressed. It was only then that I realised that I had already been in the kundalini process for almost 20 years. Talk about a light-bulb going on!

I then continued to raise the kundalini in a gentler way and without the breathing component and that worked much better for me. My head chakra opened more and more and, as I have described in the introduction, I was rewarded with greatly increased clairvoyance, which I mainly used to get answers to my many metaphysical questions. I also developed more classical kundalini symptoms like regular experiences of rising heat in my spine and numerous energy experiences in my chakras, sometimes as pain but more often as the different facets of bliss.

But the rest of my life did not go to plan. For some reason I seemed to lose my manifesting abilities and my entire life seemed to grind to a halt that lasted for almost eight years.

I developed much over-sensitivity - of which aversion to noise was the most prominent - and felt very alienated from my surroundings. In fact, I felt so alienated that my husband and I made plans to emigrate from England and we explored several countries to move to. Unfortunately, practical considerations did not allow us to make these plans a reality and eventually we simply moved a bit further away from London. But doing so meant that I had to give up meditation group and my counselling practice. I planned to spend my time writing my books instead but to my dismay the publishers were not interested in any more books from me, so I was left practically without work, which I did not like at all.

To make matters even more challenging, the relationship with my husband needed a complete overhaul because I was rapidly developing under the influence of the kundalini and he was not. Due to my clairvoyant abilities, I became able to look deeply into his unconscious mind and what I saw was not pretty. Needless to say, my husband was not very enthusiastic about these developments, either. But with time he accepted my newfound wisdom and embraced his own development on a deeper level.

My health, which had always been bad, deteriorated even further and I developed numerous aches and pains and other debilitating symptoms like chronic coughs and feeling terribly hot and cold over extended periods of time. For over two years I suffered from textbook-like symptoms of gallbladder disease that gave me great pain, yet an ultrasound scan revealed that my gallbladder was in perfect order. On another occasion I developed a debilitating ulcer-like stomach pain that lasted on and off for another two years.

During these eight years I became more and more housebound because there was less and less that interested me beyond my meditation and metaphysical explorations. All my previous friendships came to an end because I was simply not on the same wavelength with my various friends anymore. It happened gently and without falling out with anyone but, apart from my husband (and very occasionally Garchen Rinpoche), I could not make myself feel understood by anyone throughout these years. So I had very few contacts during this time and relied more and more heavily on the 'conversations' that I had with White Tara.

On the rare occasions that I did go out, I felt so over-sensitive that the sight of litter at the roadside made me physically gag and the noise that goes on wherever there are people about felt like a hammering on my head. I even had to give up my beloved country walks due to the incessant aeroplane noise in the South-East of England, which was quite a hard blow for me. And when we tried going on a family holiday, I was overcome with strange stressful feelings that ruined the whole experience for me. As time went on, I started to worry whether I had 'lost the plot' and whether I was actually going mad instead of developing spiritually. However, in White Tara's readings she continuously reassured me that this was not the case.

All this sounds quite dramatic and miserable but I was far from unhappy during that time. My soul continued to be saturated with bliss and ecstasy every day for several hours. Rivers of the sweetest and most delicious feelings were meandering through my body, going up in the front of my body and down my spine or into my arms and legs accompanied by beautiful visions of opening flowers. The bliss was so intense that it can only be called orgasmic but it was much sweeter and more all-pervading than an ordinary orgasm. Due to the ecstasy, my body contorted into rapturous postures to give expression to these most exalted feelings, mostly through gestures in my hands (called *mudras*).

Sights like a flowering garden propelled me into ecstatic feelings of gratitude and bliss so intense that tears started rolling down my cheeks. Even ordinary objects like the back of chair appeared so beautiful that the sight of them was as enrapturing as the sight of a new lover. The same happened with music that at times appeared as coming directly from heaven and having a dimension of bliss and hope that alleviated all suffering. At other times, I felt as if all the birds flying around were really angels sent by God to do some heavenly errands reminding us of a dimension that is so remote for many people.

At times these wonderful feelings spontaneously expressed themselves in poems and songs emerging from the depth of my soul and I took up the hobby of embroidering pictures of enlightened beings in thousands of hours of work. It deeply inspired and satisfied me to see these enlightened beings coming to life through the threads of my needle.

I had many truly awesome spiritual experiences that transformed the way I related to the divine and the world in the most profound and wonderful ways. The crowning of these spiritual experiences came when I started to feel truly merged with the divine for longer and longer periods of time feeling that my old personality had been erased and replaced with the divine presence of White Tara. I was also blessed with genuine divine visitations both in dreams and in daylight. It was then that Garchen Rinpoche asked me to teach others and gave me his blessings for all my unpublished books.

During these years I spent a large portion of my time taking down readings from White Tara almost on a daily basis by asking random questions. Doing this was both exhilarating and a bit painful. White Tara never gave me long lectures but only ever answered succinctly. So, when I wanted to find out about a certain metaphysical field I had to ask hundreds of questions before I felt the whole topic had been covered.

Interestingly, asking all these questions was not very pleasurable. In order to ask questions I had to doubt what I had known before and approach these readings with an unknowing mind. But nobody likes their worldview pulled apart and I was no exception. Every new question and every short answer was like opening a can of worms, showing me just how ignorant I was about the nature of who and what we are, which was rather uncomfortable to say the least.

But over the years I began to expand into the deepest metaphysical secrets of the universe and a coherent picture slowly emerged. In the beginning I did not take these teachings very seriously because I did not believe that I should *really* have the ability to communicate with a divine being. I simply thought that these readings were a way of tapping into my own intuition. But slowly I became convinced by the genuineness of my readings because there was never a contradiction within the answers to all these random questions that had meandered this way and that way like a massive sprawling city.

Much of what White Tara dictated to me was new to me and by going back over my journals I could see that I asked the same questions over and over again only to receive the same answer over and over, as well. I took this as another sign that I did not make these readings up myself. Surely I wouldn't have asked the same questions up to 15 times if I had known the answer already.

I spent much time ordering these chaotic readings into a systematic manuscript, which I had to re-structure numerous times as new information emerged. Up to the present date, I have collected over 250 pages of the most condense and concise bullet points, which I have structured into numerous headings, subheadings and sub-sub-headings.

I found great solace in these readings and White Tara's words guided me through all the problems and pitfalls of these years. Most of all, she reassured me that there was nothing wrong with me being stuck at home most of the time because all mystics have to take refuge in the solitude of remote hermitages at some point in their development.

I also conducted numerous readings on personal questions and concerns about my family, which were very helpful. For example, I had quite a few worries about bringing up my son, who had been born prematurely, and I also asked questions about other practical issues. White Tara always gave me short and succinct predictions but it took me years before I trusted these readings. Looking back over many years of these predictions, I can say with hand on my heart that they all came true. Often the timing was out by a few weeks but the thrust of the message was always spot-on. Here is just one example:

As I said, during these years I found it virtually impossible to find a new publisher. In fact, it took me years to even find an agent. Once I had finally found an agent, she tried very hard to sell one of my books but informed me after six months that she was unable to do so and cancelled her contract with me. Obviously, I was upset about yet another setback and seriously considered giving up getting published entirely. But when I asked White Tara she said simply and succinctly: 'This is the low-point; from now on it will go upwards.' But with the best will of the world I could not imagine how my publishing situation could improve as I had no intention of trying anything new. But six weeks later my now ex-agent emailed me and told me that she had been approached by a reputable publisher asking her whether she had any exciting proposals. My agent offered my manuscript to the publisher who was excited and willing to publish it. So, my situation had indeed turned around from a seemingly hopeless situation. Several more predictions White Tara made for me which appeared similarly unlikely also came true nevertheless.

The only thing that really upset me during this time was that I did not have enough students and clients to pass my knowledge on to and that I felt that all my bliss was somehow wasted if I could not teach it to others.

I still worked with a small number of clients, mostly over the phone, but I had the desire to reach more people to make them aware of the healing secrets that had been revealed to me. Since my discovery of higher-consciousness healing seven years ago, client after client had achieved the most wondrous healings from lifelong problems like anxiety, depression, fatigue and relationships problems within weeks. In the years before my discovery of this method I had only limited effect on the well-being of my clients, yet now I was able to show my clients how to heal themselves within weeks and months and free themselves from the most debilitating problems.

I had the same successes once I started working with kundalini clients because I discovered that they responded equally well to higher-consciousness healing as my regular clients. I believe that the reason for this is that higher consciousness uses pure love as the healing agent and that this love pacifies the out-of-control life force during a kundalini awakening.

As a result of my years of channelling and meditating, I had also become much more clairvoyant and knowledgeable about what would help each individual client and became more and more adept at tailor-making a meditation for each client that would address and heal their most important problem. So, I complained to White Tara that all her knowledge she had given me would be wasted if she did not help me to pass it on to more people.

It was then that White Tara urged me to write this book, although I resisted it for several years. I simply thought that kundalini is too risky to teach openly and, to a degree, I also lacked confidence.

White Tara explained to me that my problems were due to the fact that I had not managed to bring the kundalini evenly into all my chakras. My 'noise problem' and the pain in my midriff were due to blocks in my solar plexus chakra, she said, and my bad health and lack of professional success was due to a blocked navel chakra.

I took White Tara's advice to heart and made a great effort to practice with these chakras because I had seen how opening my heart, throat and head chakras had led to significant improvements in my emotional wellbeing, as well as in the outer circumstances of my life. But my two lower chakras remained stubbornly blocked for quite a while.

But once I had accumulated enough kundalini in my navel and solar plexus chakras, my fortunes turned yet again. The first thing that improved was my health. After suffering virtually all my adult life with chronic inflammations and numerous symptoms, I became well virtually overnight. What is even more astounding, I have stayed completely well ever since for the last five years. (That had been another of White Tara's predictions that I could not believe.)

Then, literally from one day to the next, I was suddenly flooded with clients who found me through my website which had been languishing virtually unnoticed on the Internet. Suddenly, and without me having made any changes, a large number of people contacted me and asked to be my clients. Needless to say, I was overjoyed.

I very much loved working with my clients and continued to have the same positive results that I have described above with both my kundalini clients, as well as my regular clients. As an added bonus, my increased income made it possible for us to move into an isolated house in a remote part of England and I finally found the peace and quiet in a hermitage that I had craved so badly for years.

I continue to have the bliss and ecstasy that I have described above but nowadays I frequently have experiences in which my inner bliss merges with what I see around myself and I truly experience this very world as a paradise.

I have to admit that do not really like to talk too much about all the bliss and rapture that I experience because I could be accused of 'spiritual boasting'. However, I have been very honest about the difficulties I have experienced to give you an idea about what could happen during a kundalini awakening and I think it is equally important to tell you about all the riches and blessings that are at the heart of a kundalini awakening. For myself, the joys and blessings have far outweighed the challenging side of the kundalini and the purpose of this book is to help you trust, and also to experience, that your own kundalini awakening can be equally positive and rewarding.

Are you ready for your kundalini awakening?

If you have followed all the preparatory steps so far, you are now ready to awaken the kundalini. Let me repeat what this preparation ideally represents:

Check-list of whether you are ready to awaken the kundalini

You have checked your motivation and you want to awaken the kundalini with the sole goal of reaching enlightenment and helping others.

You have seriously considered the impact of having a kundalini awakening and you are sure you are ready to deal with anything it may bring up.

You are free of chronic negative emotions like strong anxiety, depression or anger.

You are free of chronic pain and fatigue.

Your personal relationships are in good shape and you have people around you with whom you can talk about the intimate details of your life.

You do not suffer from any form of sexual dysfunction and you do not practice any form of sexual acts that could be physically or psychologically hurtful for anybody.

You do not harbour any chronic resentment against anybody.

Your life-style is generally healthy.

Your sleeping pattern is good.

You have practised loving-kindness meditation and witness consciousness for at least a year on most days.

You have a devoted relationship to your higher power.

You have opened the top four chakras and you can feel a sense of wellbeing in all four top chakras on a regular basis.

If the above list appears too long and too demanding to you, remember that whatever unresolved issues you have will be amplified once kundalini is present. It really makes sense to sort things out *before* the strong energy of kundalini 'forces you' through pain to deal with them.

We will now come to various ways to awaken the kundalini. Some of these approaches are similar to the chakra awakening techniques that we have already discussed in the previous chapter and some are new.

Devotion as a means to awakening the kundalini

As you know, White Tara has always made it a strong point that devotion to your higher power is crucial in every step of your kundalini awakening. Here she explains why this is so crucial:

> *Every loving encounter produces energy – just like nuclear fusion is the fastest way to produce energy and just like the fusion of two people can produce a baby. Every fusion of two beings produces energy. If this fusion is done with love, good energy evolves.*
>
> *The best way to awaken the kundalini is to have strong devotion to a deity and to tune into the energy of the deity by meditating on the union with your higher power through the navel. You do this through the navel because this chakra can carry most energy. If you focus on the navel without devotion to the deity, nothing much will happen.*

So, in principle we are using exactly the same approach that we have been using to awaken the higher chakras. We imagine our higher power in front of us and open our navel chakra towards this wonderful being and merge our energy field with theirs at the level of the navel.

White Tara is admonishing us yet again that we should not treat the kundalini as a mechanical force that we can awaken by ourselves outside of relationships, as it can easily lead to the corruption of our ego. The best relationship to awaken the kundalini is one with a divine being or an enlightened guru.

You may wonder why White Tara places so much importance on the devotion to the divine when some kundalini teachers describe kundalini as some sort of inanimate energy that is not part of a living being.

Remember, White Tara teaches that everything that exists in the universe is part of a living being – that there is no such thing as dead matter as taught in our current scientific view of the world. In White Tara's view of the world, our kundalini energy arises through the loving encounter with someone and this someone should be the most loving and wisest being in the universe – our higher power.

The merging with a divine being can be compared with falling in love. If you have ever been truly in love, you will agree that it has been the time in your life when you felt most energetic and alive and when you were happiest. In other words, falling in love is somewhat akin to a mini kundalini awakening. In the same way, we should use the loving encounter with our higher power to generate this wonderful energy that will lead us to enlightenment.

Strong desire to serve others as a means to awaken the kundalini

You may remember that in chapter one White Tara told us that the life force is essentially desire and that kundalini is particularly concentrated desire. Therefore, the stronger our desire, the easier will be our kundalini awakening.

Obviously, we are not talking about the desire that fuels addictions because this form of desire has an in-built loop of frustration. The *only* desire we can use to awaken the kundalini is the wish to be more loving, to help others more, and generally to do more good in the world and for all beings. This wish to bring love into the world is the purest desire and it will help us to ignite our life force in the safest and most efficient way possible.

White Tara also explained that the stronger our wish to help others, the greater will be our initial disbelief that we can do it. It is this friction between our desire and our disbelief that creates the highest amount of energy. Therefore, we are encouraged to have an almost extreme desire to help others.

Working with the navel chakra

Aside from the devotion to our higher power and our desire to help others, the most important factor for a kundalini awakening is concentration on the navel chakra. Here White Tara explains why the navel chakra is most suited to awakening the kundalini:

> *Kundalini can be awakened at any chakra but the navel is most suited to it because it can tolerate more energy than all other chakras.*

The exact location of the navel chakra

When studying the literature about the kundalini it always puzzled me that there were so many different locations given for the navel chakra. Some said it is exactly in the navel and some said it is an inch or two inches below the navel. In the Hindu system the navel chakra is sometimes depicted as sitting in the solar plexus just below the rib cage, while the sacral chakra is at the level of the womb and the root chakra is at the tip of the genitals. Here is White Tara's very pragmatic answer to this question:

> *You focus foremost on the navel or somewhere in your lower abdomen, wherever you most easily feel the energy.*

So White Tara is making it really simple: we can choose the location of the navel chakra somewhere between genitals and navel, wherever we can most readily feel the energy. It can also be helpful to simply focus on the entire abdominal cavity, not forgetting to visualise our body as hollow and filled with brilliant light.

Chakras are not pre-defined 'things' like organs but originate in our mind and take on more and more physical reality as we focus on them. This means that to a certain degree we can *decide* the location of our navel chakra. Energy follows thought, so when we concentrate on a particular area in our abdomen, the energy will gather there and after some time will take on a life of its own.

Opening the navel chakra

White Tara has given us these instructions for opening the navel chakra:

> *Focus on the navel and make the energy really blissful. You can use the words: pleasure, power, success, confidence or excitement – whatever works best.*

When White Tara says 'make the energy in the navel really blissful', she means using all the chakra-opening approaches we have discussed in chapter four. Everything that has been said about how to open the higher chakras is also true for the navel chakra. Here is a short recap of the other ways to open a chakra, which will work for the navel chakra, as well:

Visualise merging with your higher power at the navel chakra.

Visualise your abdomen as hollow and filled with brilliant light and smile into the navel chakra with love.

Deeply relax the chakra through imagining a flower opening or other relaxing visualisations, stretching or massage.

Associate the navel chakra with a visualisation of whatever is your greatest wish and whatever inspires you most deeply. Make sure that this wish also serves humankind as a whole. In that way, you fulfil the requirement to focus on helping others and linking this to your navel chakra.

Associate with the navel chakra the words 'great joy', 'excited joy', 'fulfilment', 'confidence', 'inspiration' or whatever word or phrase works best for you.

Associate with the navel chakra a memory of when you felt deeply inspired, confident and motivated to do something that felt profoundly meaningful to you.

Pelvic squeezes

Apart from the techniques outlined above, there are a few additional things you can do to open the navel chakra. The first of these techniques is pelvic squeezes.

Gentle pelvic squeezes are helpful in awakening the lower chakras. These squeezes are done like stopping the flow of your urine. It is important that you do these squeezes only really gently and only periodically. Pelvic squeezes are not meant to work like a mechanical pump. As I said before, it is very important never to approach the whole topic of working with our inner energies in a mechanical way but rather with great awareness, surrender, relaxation and devotion.

So, in order to work with pelvic squeezes, you gently tighten your pelvic floor for a second or two and then let go. When you let go, you will feel a gently flow of energy. Focus on this energy, surrender to it and let it rise and unfold on its own accord without interfering. Simply observe and surrender.

Using sexual energy

We can also use sexual energy to awaken the navel chakra. This can sometimes be tricky because too much sexual energy can be difficult to bear without an orgasm to release the energy. And while White Tara does not advocate complete abstinence, she does not recommend frequent orgasms, either. Particularly for men, this can be depleting and counter-productive for awakening the kundalini. She says:

> *You may also utilise sexual energy to activate the navel chakra. Sexual*

energy is not easy to handle, so you should only do this as long as it feels comfortable.

We can utilise sexual energy by gently arousing our genital area with the heel of our foot while sitting in a cross-legged position. We can also think of our higher power in an erotic way if he or she is of our preferred gender. Doing this is a practice that has been used by Tibetan Buddhist monks and nuns as a means of arousing their kundalini. This approach is not for everyone as it may bring up deep-seated resistance to the mixing of the spiritual with the sexual. Only do it if it appeals to you.

Pulsing energy
Another way to awaken the navel chakra is to visualise and feel a sense of pulsing energy in the navel chakra. This is very similar to feeling our heartbeat when we are relaxed – whoom... whoom... whoom. Remember to keep visualising your abdomen as hollow and filled with brilliant light way when you do this and simply observe how the energy unfolds.

Persistence of focus
I have already mentioned that, ideally, we should focus all day long on the chakra we want to open. This becomes even more vital when we are working with the navel chakra because this chakra is hard to penetrate with the mind alone. The more often we can bring our mind back to the navel chakra throughout the day, the more successful we will be.

Other ways to awaken the kundalini
During my work as a kundalini therapist and also through researching the literature, I have come across a number of other ways of awakening the kundalini. As you will see, none of these methods are conducive to a conscious and safe awakening but, for completeness sake, I will mention them here:

Yvonne Kason explained that near-death experiences can lead to a kundalini awakening. Penny Sartori has written a well-researched book about the long-term effects of near-death experiences. It is interesting to read that these long-term effects are indeed virtually identical to the long-term effects of a kundalini awakening.

Extremely intense meditation retreats with night vigils and fasting.
Yvonne Kason also describes how a period of intense concentration such as when writing a PhD can awaken the kundalini.
Being struck by lightning.
One of my clients described how an intense erotic encounter that remained unconsummated awakened her kundalini.
One person I know claims her kundalini was awakened after taking a homeopathic medicine.
One person I know claims that her kundalini was awakened after a laughter workshop.

Shaktipat

Another, rather risky way to awaken the kundalini is shaktipat, which is the touch through which the kundalini is transferred from one person to another. Shaktipat is only safe if you have a deeply devoted and trusting relationship to the spiritual teacher in question. By definition, this should be a long-term relationship and you should know your teacher well enough to vouch for their integrity and purity of spiritual teaching.

Unfortunately, I have seen cases where shaktipat has been given without the express permission of the student, which led to confusion and sometimes also much resentment. There is also the danger of picking up some of the human weaknesses of a teacher when receiving shaktipat and all this can lead to much unhealthy entanglement with this person. White Tara says:

> It is important to know a person very well before receiving shaktipat. It is highly dangerous just to take it from anyone who is offering it. Do resist that temptation as it may lead to numerous problems.

Dangerous ways of awakening the kundalini

Some people find it easy to tune into the blissful energy at the navel but for others it can take a long time. The navel chakra can be more difficult to awaken than the other chakras because it is the bridge between the levels of mind and matter. If you have this difficulty, it is important to be patient and not to hurry the process through forceful methods as the repercussions of doing this can be severe. White Tara warned me repeatedly not to use forceful breathing or intensive muscular movements. She says:

> *Practices that use breath-retention and forceful muscular movements are dangerous because they are too mechanical. The point is to become divine. If you do not focus on the blissful deity-state, you are missing the point.*
>
> *There are certain ways to manipulate your energy system and take shortcuts, for example, by reversing your sexuality and doing extreme things, but these are unsafe and will bring unhappiness. They work by focusing into extreme states of mind that usually stay hidden from your consciousness. The shock of the experience dislodges the kundalini. It is not good to work that way.*

The rising of the kundalini

Once we have focused on the navel with the techniques we have discussed in the previous sections for long enough, two things will happen. Firstly, the pleasure in our abdomen will turn into heat. The second thing is that there will be a sensation of pleasure and heat rising up in our body. For some people this development may happen within hours of starting the navel practice while for others it may take many months of concentrated effort, depending on their disposition. White Tara says:

> *When the life force becomes very strong and concentrated, it is felt as a blissful warmth or heat that starts in your abdomen and enlarges from there to connect all your chakras along the spine in the central channel.*

In the textbooks kundalini is often described as a hot energy that is slowly ascending up the spine. But in my work as a kundalini therapist I have found that the picture is a bit more variable than that. Some of my clients had an almost textbook-like experience of the kundalini starting in their abdomen and then slowly rising, chakra after chakra, to the head in one gigantic overwhelming experience. However, in many of my clients the kundalini has worked in a gentler and less straightforward way. For example, sometimes the kundalini rises within a split-second in one short whoosh, after which one finds oneself bathed in golden, blissful light surrounding the head. Other people never had a clear experience of the kundalini rising but have all the symptoms that show that their kundalini is active.

When working with the exercises in this book, you are most likely to experience the second variety of the kundalini rising swiftly within a split second. If the experience was strong enough, you may then feel the energy slowly travelling down your body again.

Practicing in this way is much safer than having the one-off freight train like experience that some of my clients have had. But if you had a stronger experience, do not panic - you might be able to cope with it just fine.

Helpful visualisations

In order to facilitate the upward movement of energy, you can visualise a flower opening upwards in your lower abdomen. You will remember that we have used an image of a flower opening outward in order to open all the chakras. Now we simply imagine that the flower bud points upwards into our body towards the head.

Another helpful visualisation is imagining a hot bright flame in our abdomen and when the energy starts to rise up we see this flame rising up as well and enlarging into a long thin hot flame.

My own favourite image is of a flower with its roots in the navel, the stem along the spine and flowers opening out at the various chakras and my hands.

The nature of the central channel

You may remember that we have already discussed in chapter four how White Tara refutes the traditional textbook idea that kundalini literally rises up in our body along the spine. Instead, she says that the central channel only appears like a holographic image when the lower chakras get purified.

Why does White Tara emphasise so much that a kundalini rising is just an impression rather than a real event? The answer is that she tries to warn us, yet again, not to manipulate this experience or to think about it too materialistically. The key is to focus on our mind, to surrender and to let it happen. She says:

> *This sense of rising and expanding of the kundalini is the actual kundalini awakening and you should always practice in this way. However, the 'rising of energy' is just a sensation and is not real. There are no channels or pathways. You do not fabricate a stream of energy and you do not try to move anything. You just notice how it happens automatically.*
>
> *Just surrender to this energy and notice how a 'stream of energy' 'rises up' from the navel. This feeling enlarges up the spine and over your whole body*

and fills you with intense pleasure and a feeling of inexhaustible energy and power. This is the light-body.

Imagine the energy in the form of the white egg enveloping your entire body and not only in small channels and points.

You should try to accumulate as much kundalini as possible by surrendering to the energy in your abdomen and letting it expand from there. However, just like 'energy' and 'rising up', the word 'accumulating' is only a manner of speaking. What it refers to is the stabilised awareness of the kundalini.

The pathway of the rising kundalini

White Tara also gave me teachings about where exactly in the body the kundalini rises up (even though this is not an actual rising). She says:

The sensation of the kundalini along the spine may come and go in the beginning. Also, you may experience the 'pathway' of the kundalini as straight or curved at the head or you may feel the kundalini going along the spine or more in the middle of the body. All this is less important.

However, White Tara warns about letting the kundalini 'rise' in the front of the body. She says:

In the front of the body kundalini can burn the soft tissue of the organs. The nerve tissue in the spine is made to withstand these frequencies. Once you are accustomed to kundalini you can feel the central channel in the middle of your body and finally spread the kundalini throughout your whole body.

So, in order to ensure that the kundalini 'rises' in the spine, gently focus on your back when you do the navel practice. The kundalini will then automatically take the safer 'pathway' up the spine. If you can do this without any problems, you can experiment to let the kundalini rise up in the middle of your body and see how that feels.

Heat and bliss must stay together

Whenever we let the kundalini rise, we need to make sure that the experience of heat stays connected with the experience of bliss. White Tara teaches about the sensation of heat:

> *Kundalini is a mild electromagnetic current and just like an electric cable it gets warm if there is a lot of energy. However, there is more to kundalini than electricity. Kundalini also includes the finer spiritual vibrations of your divine essence, including the very finest.*
>
> *Ideally, during the kundalini experience heat and pleasure should stay combined because heat on its own is dangerous – it always needs to be merged with the sea of love and bliss or else it can burn your chakras and inner organs and increase your negative ego. Love and kundalini always need to grow simultaneously.*
>
> *If kundalini gets divorced from love, it is greatly ego strengthening and will also increase all sorts of negative emotions. Therefore, your practice should always be conducted with a focus on love and bliss. This will be your greatest safeguard.*
>
> *Sometimes the heat is felt in one part of the body, for example the spine, and the bliss is somewhere else, for example in the front of the body, and that is okay.*
>
> *The colour of the kundalini is a brilliant white or at least golden. Seeing this light with your inner eye is important because it makes sure that the heat stays connected to your divine essence. The clearer and brighter the light, the better – it indicates higher and better vibrations. You must resist dark colours because they contain negative energy.*
>
> *When you have reached the highest state, the experience of heat will stop but your powers will be greatly enhanced.*

The spreading of the kundalini
The final development of the kundalini is the spreading out of the energy into your environment. As emphasised many times before, this development should occur naturally and spontaneously and we should not push and try to manufacture this

experience. When the kundalini goes into your environment, imagine that it brings healing and spiritual happiness to countless beings. White Tara explains:

> *Finally, the whole universe is filled with your light and warmth - like from a star. Remember, nothing 'spreads' and 'fills' – you are just gradually increasing your vibrations.*
>
> *When the blissful kundalini goes into your environment, it 'changes' it into the experience of a paradise. Everything pulsates in the same blissful rhythm. The whole universe is filled with your light and warmth - like from a star.*

Needless to say, this is the most amazing state of mind and it is easy to see that a number people who have experienced it have been mistaken in believing that they were enlightened. However, in order to reach enlightenment we need more than kundalini – we also need to merge with the mind of the deity, which is pure love. It is this balance of kundalini bliss and divine love that is enlightenment and not the kundalini bliss alone. We will discuss how to reach this final state in chapter seven.

Possible challenges when the kundalini rises

When the kundalini 'rises up' it will amplify every tension or faulty belief that we hold in all the higher chakras. The more thoroughly we have done our preparation as described in chapters three and four, the fewer problems we will experience. However, our chakras are as 'vast and deep' as our unconscious mind, so we should be prepared for some further problem areas to surface.

If we encounter a problem by way of negative emotions or pain at one of the higher chakras, we should discontinue our focus on our navel and work on opening the affected chakra first. This can take anything from a few minutes to a few months. I will go into much more depth about how to work with kundalini problems in the next chapter.

The complete practice of awakening the kundalini

Here is the complete practice for awakening your kundalini. It is very similar to the chakra awakening practice that you have already done in chapter four. However, you should only practice with the navel chakra once you have mastered opening all the higher chakras:

Exercise: Awakening the kundalini
Preparation
Resolve to awaken the kundalini for the best of all beings.
Imagine your higher power in front of you filled and surrounded by beautiful light. Your higher power is smiling at you with deepest love and wishes you to be happy and enlightened.
Visualise your body as hollow and filled with brilliant light.
Mentally go to the top four chakras in your body and open them as you have learnt in chapter four.

Opening the navel chakra
Bring to mind your strong desire to reach enlightenment for the sake of all beings. Feel this desire burning like a flame in your lower abdomen. Feel and see this flame anywhere between the navel and the genitals where you feel most energy.
Work with the navel chakra with one or all of the following approaches, whatever works best:
Smile into the navel chakra with love.
Deeply *relax* the navel chakra through imagining a flower opening.
Merge the navel chakra with your higher power.
Support the navel opening with gentle and occasional pelvic squeezes and surrender to the pleasant feelings that doing this evokes.
If you can handle sexual energy, use whatever image or touch you like to evoke this energy and allow it to make the feeling at your navel stronger and hotter.
Imagine a pulsation in your navel chakra until you can actually feel it.
If you feel numbness or physical tensions in the navel chakra, try stretching and massaging your abdomen.
When you experience a positive feeling in your navel chakra, associate it with a word, image or memory so that it will be easier to recall.
Focus on the sense of wellbeing in the navel chakra and refrain from trying to manipulate this feeling in any way. Simply observe it and notice how it expands and rises on its own accord.
If you experience any distracting thoughts and feelings, simply let them go and come back to your pleasant feeling at the navel over and over again.

The rising of the kundalini

Once you have focused on the navel chakra for some time you will feel a sense of heat. It is important to retain the feeling of wellbeing once the heat starts.

There will also be a spontaneous sense of rising of the bliss and the heat. Do not try to raise the kundalini yourself but let it happen on its own accord. It may take days, weeks or months for this to happen.

Once you feel the first rising of the energy, facilitate it by visualising a flower bud in your abdomen that opens upwards towards your head or as a flame that enlarges towards your head.

If you feel any discomfort, focus more on the spine because this is the safer pathway.

At some point the kundalini along the spine enlarges to form an egg-shaped light ball around your body. Let this happen spontaneously and simply observe it.

Eventually, the kundalini will expand into your environment and you will shine like a beautiful star. When this happens imagine that the light of your kundalini goes to countless beings and brings them healing and spiritual happiness.

Whenever you find yourself distracted by wandering thoughts, come back to the navel, focus on the heat and bliss there and allow the energy to rise again.

If you feel any negative feelings in one of the other chakras, stop the focus on the navel chakra and work with the 'problem chakra' until it is open and blissful again. This can take minutes, several days or even weeks.

Ending the meditation
End your meditation by dedicating all its benefits to the best of all beings.

Symptoms of a kundalini awakening

After some time spent working with your inner energies, you will start developing the typical kundalini symptoms outlined below. They may happen suddenly or very gradually at an unpredictable rate. Some people will develop these symptoms after practising for only a few days, while for others it may take years. Also, you may not experience all the symptoms but only some of them.

Here is a list of the many symptoms you may experience over the years after you have had a kundalini awakening. Some of these symptoms we have already discussed in chapter two. It is important to remember that kundalini symptoms are not 'new' to our system but merely an amplification of our old self. Every positive and negative part of us will be enlarged and more noticeable and therefore there is nothing to be afraid of:

Mental and spiritual kundalini symptoms

Comfortable

Feeling drawn to spiritual practice and literature
Stronger motivation to make one's life-style healthier and more loving and spiritual in every respect
Motivation to work in a profession where you can be of service to others
Motivation to spend time in nature and live in a natural setting
Heightened intuition, deeper wisdom and even clairvoyance
Ability to make deeper contact with your higher power
Ingenious insights and heightened creativity
Heightened ability to access one's own unconscious mind and see the positive and negative character traits of oneself and other people more realistically
Inspiring past life memories
Heightened ability to progress on one's chosen spiritual path, understand spiritual literature and experience exalted spiritual states
Increased ability to be honest, humble and to laugh about oneself
Heightened ability to feel other people's emotions and read their minds
Increased ability and power to influence others (also called charisma)
Increased power to manifest our desires
Development of supernatural powers like spiritual healing
Hearing of heavenly music or sounds
Seeing beautiful lights, sights, visions and colours
Experiencing ordinary objects and people as intensely beautiful

Uncomfortable

Increased problems with irrational thinking and confusion, e.g. intensified neurotic thought patterns or faulty spiritual concepts
Episodes of increased selfishness, pride or even megalomania (e.g. believing one is Christ)
Episodes of unrealistic low self-esteem
Making impulsive decisions based on confused assumptions
Hearing of (frightening) voices and disagreeable sounds
Disturbing past life memories
Seeing frightening visions like contorted faces in the dark, ghosts and demons

Emotional kundalini symptoms

Comfortable

Deep states of bliss and ecstasy
Deep and effortless love, forgiveness and compassion towards friends and enemies alike
Fewer needs for emotional support from others and fewer material needs and desires
Deep humility but also unshakeable self-confidence and compassion for oneself
Increased motivation and ability to give up negative and addictive habits
Seeing other people's inner beauty and their potential to be divine

Uncomfortable

Amplified negative emotions like strong anxiety, despair and anger
Emotions may become so strong that they feel like physical pain
Discovery of negative emotions that one was unaware of before - like envy, spitefulness, racism and hatred
Amplified feelings of guilt
Amplified sexual issues
Resurgence of old emotional traumas and wounds
General oversensitivity to sense stimuli like noise, bright light or simply 'vibrations', e.g. one may enter a house and find the atmosphere intolerable
Fear of going mad
Amplification of relationship problems, feelings of not being able to relate to family members or old friends anymore
Seeing other people's selfish motivations more clearly
Sense of alienation from the world

Physical kundalini symptoms

Comfortable

Sense of pleasurable energy rising from the abdomen
Deep sense of physical bliss, e.g. orgasmic feelings all over one's body
Better health and resistance to illness
Increased beauty, radiance and physical rejuvenation (e.g. wrinkles disappear)
Spontaneous blissful movements (so-called kriyas)
Sexual feelings all over the body (some people find that very uncomfortable)
Feeling more sexual in a positive way, e.g. massively intensified orgasms

Higher amount of physical energy
Urge to change one's diet and life-style to be healthier

Uncomfortable
Tingling, buzzing, tickling sensations all over the body
Jerking, shaking, quivering
Weird body sensations like feeling that parts of one's body are unusually enlarged
Resurgence of old or chronic pain and disease
Unexplained sudden pains in many areas of the body: stabbing, burning, gnawing pains
Untreatable chronic pain that is not related to any diagnosable illness
Sense of uncomfortable churning energy
Sense of 'too much' energy moving through one's body, often up the spine
Sense of energy blocks, e.g. sense of energy collecting in areas of the body and causing discomfort and pain
Textbook-like symptoms of well-known diseases that cannot be found by a doctor
Over-sensitivity and more pronounced side effects of prescription drugs and complementary medicine
Head pressure
Increase or decrease in appetite and the need for food
Hot flushes or sensations of coldness
Uncomfortable spontaneous body movements
Strongly increased or decreased libido, embarrassing new sexual desires or change of sexual orientation
Low energy and fatigue
Insomnia

Long-term development of kundalini awakening

Many clients ask me how long a kundalini experience will last and hope that the answer will be that it will be only a short event after which they will be able to return to their old way of life. But this is not how it will happen - if anything, we will grow *into* the experience.

Kundalini is not a disease that will flare up and then go away again. It is much more akin to puberty. It will awaken a certain quality or function within us that, once awakened, is here to stay. If we were to fight our sex drive, we would create many physiological and neurotic problems and inhibit our healthy development.

The same is true for a kundalini awakening. The more we fight it, the more difficult and complicated it will be. And the more we embrace this experience and proactively deal with all its challenges, the more rewarding the experience will be.

Let's remind ourselves that the real purpose of a kundalini awakening is to reach enlightenment as rapidly as possible. Once we are on this track, there is no turning back and our development will not stop until the end of our life. Probably it will go on into our future lives as well in which we may experience an early and possibly involuntary kundalini awakening. Yvonne Kason identified four major patterns of kundalini development in her book Farther Shores:

A slow, gradual increase of kundalini and spiritual experiences occurring over many years

Episodes of profound kundalini and spiritual experiences separated by episodes of few or no experiences

Episodes of profound kundalini and spiritual experiences separated by periods of gradually increasing kundalini and spiritual experiences

One profound kundalini experience followed by a slow and gradual increase of experiences

My own life has followed the first pattern but most of my clients follow the third and last patterns. The more profound your initial experience is, the more it will shatter your previous outlook and approach to life and the more it has the potential to leave you frightened and confused. It is understandable to wish to go back to how you were before but it is important to realise that this will not happen. Let me express this more positively: in my opinion having a kundalini awakening is like winning the lottery. For the unprepared mind, this may lead to confusion and reckless behaviour but it is nevertheless the best thing that could happen to anyone.

Chapter six
Dealing with the Challenges of a Kundalini Awakening

Kundalini is the prerequisite to achieving and stabilising enlightenment, yet we have seen that it can cause many uncomfortable side effects. It is fair to ask why it should cause so many problems if it is meant to be such a fortunate event. This is a valid question that we will be looking at in detail in the next few sections.

Generally speaking, most people first experience the wonderful side of a kundalini awakening with all its inherent bliss and spiritual insights. Some weeks or months later the more problematic side comes to the fore and there may be all sorts of uncomfortable kundalini symptoms. Father Paisios, a Greek orthodox priest living on Mount Athos in retreat, is world-renowned for his many incredible supernatural abilities like spiritual healing and clairvoyance. He described this dynamic is this most charming way: *'first you get a cookie from God's bakery shop – this is how he lures you in. Then he gives you work to do.'*

Where do kundalini problems come from and how long will they last?

It is helpful to see all kundalini problems as our own amplified conflicts. I have mentioned the following quote of White Tara already in chapter two but I will repeat it here because it explains well where our kundalini problems come from:

> All physical and psychological problems resulting from kundalini awakening are the result of your contradictory intentions. There is no kundalini energy that moves around in you on its own accord and creates problems. There is only the friction between your more loving and more selfish desires that fight with each other.

Seeing all our problems during a kundalini process as our amplified inner conflicts has several advantages. First of all, it prevents us from ever perceiving ourselves as the victim of outside forces that we cannot control. This will decrease possible feelings of depression, anger or self-pity.

Secondly, the view that all kundalini problems come from our own mind reduces fear about the many weird and wonderful experiences we may have. If we know, for example, that frightening visions of dark forces are simply our own amplified thoughts and feelings, then we do not need to be so afraid anymore.

And thirdly, the knowledge that kundalini problems have arisen from our own mind will make us feel more motivated and empowered to deal with all the problems we may encounter.

Basically, the kundalini process opens our unconscious mind so that all our unconscious conflicts and negative impulses can emerge and be cleared out. This view is in keeping with White Tara's explanation that kundalini is essentially awareness, which simply makes us conscious of our personal material that was previously suppressed in our unconscious mind.

One of my clients said to me, 'I feel that the kundalini is making me more *me* – an amplified version of myself'. I totally agree and would add that sometimes it is not very comfortable to see ourselves more deeply because we may discover parts of our mind that are embarrassing - for instance megalomaniac or sexist ideas. The task here is to respond to these thoughts and feelings with compassion, humour and of course with a firm resolution not to act on them. Simply being aware of our darker side is healing in itself since awareness itself drives us to higher stages of consciousness. On the other hand, the harder we try to suppress this emerging material, the more it will manifest as psychosomatic symptoms.

In summary, all kundalini problems come down to one central conflict and that is the battle between egotism and love. And as soon as we learn to love all beings equally – ourselves included - all kundalini problems will greatly subside. Therefore, the kundalini itself is never the problem – it is simply our inability to reconcile our contradictory impulses that causes all of our symptoms.

How long will kundalini challenges go on for?

The simple answer to this question is: forever. But please do not panic because this does not mean that you will be in a state of great suffering forever. The positive rewards of kundalini with all its bliss, supernatural powers and deep wisdom will go on forever, as well, and even grow over time. I myself have been in the kundalini process for almost 30 years and my life has only ever become better. Obviously, I had to work through my own personal challenges and I did not always get what I wanted at the click of a finger but my overall experience of life has only ever become happier, more successful and more meaningful.

I have already mentioned that our chakras are as deep and wide as our unconscious mind. In the beginning, the rising kundalini will throw up the biggest problems and this initial confusion will hopefully settle down within a few months or a year depending on how much self-development work we have already done.

After that, things may calm somewhat but we should be prepared for an ongoing process of accelerated learning and development for as long as we live. When I speak to my clients, I like to compare this process to being invited into a 'gifted class' at school. Kundalini is a privilege just like being invited into a gifted class but - just as in school - there will be more 'homework' to do and the teachers will be stricter.

Garma Chang offers us these words of comfort in his book 'Teachings and Practice of Tibetan Tantra' on pages 78 and 79: *"So in the course of Dumo [kundalini] practice, when the yogi concentrates on these Cakras, his Prana-Mind also gathers there. The concentration of the Prana-Mind on these key-syllables will spontaneously stir up the desire passions, which the bijas represent. As a result, the yogi will feel all the great passions, such as lust, hatred, doubt, pride etc., arising freely and without his own volition. All kinds of distressing and distracting thoughts and sicknesses will arise, thus impeding his devotion. Because of the concentration of Prana-Mind in the Cakras, he will also have a variety of delusory visions in dreams, in meditation, or in the waking state…. He should know that all these hindrances are actually helps, and good signs of his devotion, indicating that he is definitely making progress on the Path. Thus he should congratulate himself and gladly accept the challenge."*

General guidelines on dealing with kundalini problems

In this section I will outline the general guidelines I use in working with my kundalini clients. My approach has been very effective and usually my clients feel much better and more in control within a few months.

Slow down spiritual practices

The very first and most important advice to anyone in a kundalini crisis is to slow down all spiritual practices as these practices will heat up your kundalini process and aggravate your symptoms. Any more meditation (apart from short periods of the meditations described below) is likely to bring up more kundalini and with it more material from the unconscious mind. Therefore, when it comes to a kundalini crisis the old saying of 'less is more' is very apt.

In an acute crisis I would recommend that you only practice loving-kindness, the anti-anxiety technique, witness consciousness and devotion to your higher power as outlined below. And even these practices should not be used for more than 20 minutes a day at the very most.

I have seen many of my clients worsen their kundalini symptoms by using practices that aggravate instead of help them. This is especially the case with most forms of breathing exercises, with all sorts of energy practices or anything that is forceful and pushy like forcefully expressing emotions.

Focus on loving-kindness
We have learnt in chapter one that enlightenment is the perfect balance of love and life force/kundalini. So, if our kundalini runs out of control, the natural antidote is to focus more on love. Therefore, all practices that focus on love and kindness as explained in chapter three are beneficial for alleviating all problems caused by too much kundalini.

It cannot be overstated how important it is to be patient and kind to yourself during a difficult kundalini awakening. Any form of self-criticism and self-loathing will be greatly amplified by the kundalini process - just like all our other emotions. It is very important to resist these tendencies and be as patient and accepting of your process as you can. You need to embrace whatever is happening within you with a positive attitude and not resist whatever challenge you may experience. White Tara says:

> *You will be drawn into your old cravings over and over again until you can finally let them go. One can't hurry that process just like you cannot hurry the process of falling in love and therefore you need patience and persistence.*

Learn how to reduce fear and anxiety
Virtually all of my kundalini clients have high levels of anxiety and therefore we usually start with the anti-anxiety technique that I will outline below. I have done this exercise with hundreds of people who were suffering from the most severe anxiety and it has never failed to work within minutes.

Exercise: Anti-anxiety technique
Imagine yourself sitting in the lap of your higher power leaning back on their chest. If you like, you can also feel yourself being embraced by your higher

power. See light coming from your higher power enveloping you in a bubble of loving light. Tune in with the love of your higher power and wish yourself to be happy and healed as if you were your own best friend.

Breathe in through your nose naturally (NOT deeply) to the count of 1,2,3 and breathe out naturally through your nose (not forced in any way) to the count of 4,5,6. Then hold your breath on empty lungs and continue counting as far as possible 7,8,9,10,11,12,...20,21... (make sure you are not breathing in inadvertently). Repeat over and over to establish a rhythm. The longer the break after the out-breath, the sooner your anxiety will calm down. It is important to breathe naturally and not particularly deeply.

Notice where in your body you feel the fear and imagine this area as a tight flower bud. On the out-breath (count 4,5,6) imagine the flower bud opening and on the break after the out-breath (7,8...20...) imagine beautiful light radiating out from your open flower towards the ends of the universe. Follow the light going into infinity and relax the area of your body where the anxiety manifests. Repeat over and over but do not imagine the flower closing on the in-breath. During inhalation do nothing. Then open the flower again when you exhale.

Use this breathing and simple visualisation every time a little bit of anxiety manifests in order to nip the emotion in the bud *before* it becomes big and harder to manage. Do this exercise daily for 10 minutes and throughout the day as you need it and you will soon be able to control your fears. After a few weeks or maybe two months you will rarely need to use the technique anymore.

Practice witness consciousness

We have already discussed in chapter three the importance of being able to observe your inner thoughts, feelings and images, instead of identifying with them. Witness consciousness becomes even more important once the kundalini brings up frightening and confusing material from your unconscious mind.

If you feel particularly challenged by what is going on in your mind, try to imagine it is like a zoo full of peculiar animals. These animals are the content of your mind and you are the visitor to the zoo. The animals (your thoughts and feelings) can be weird, frightening and even dangerous but you never get into their cages and start fighting with them (which means you never try to fight with your thoughts and emotions). You always stay safely on the visitor path and observe them through tough glass or strong fences. So, you always *watch* your thoughts and emotions but you do not identify with them.

Even if the animals (your thought and feelings) seem friendly and pleasant, you never climb into their pens. This means that you do not allow yourself to be swept away by any of your emotions, even the beautiful ones. You always maintain your observer position.

Another way of practicing witness consciousness is saying out loud what is going on in your mind while you are observing it or writing it down in your journal.

Have devotion to a spiritual teacher and your higher power

It is very important to deepen your devotion and trust in your higher power and to talk to them in times of anguish and confusion. Even, if you do not always get an answer that you understand, you can be assured that your prayers will be heard. White Tara explains:

> *It is important to progress slowly and not push yourself to develop more kundalini than you can tolerate. You also need to be full of humility and devotion towards your guru. The more you can do all that, the fewer problems you will have.*

As I have outlined in chapter three, it is important to know who you can turn to *before* you run into trouble with your kundalini awakening. You do not need to find an enlightened guru to talk to; you can also try to find a kundalini therapist like myself if you run into trouble or, at the very minimum, a sympathetic psychotherapist who is open to the idea of spirituality.

Join a spiritual community of your liking

A number of my clients have experienced a kundalini awakening without being part of a spiritual community. Others have experienced a kundalini awakening while being on their first retreat with a community they have just joined and then withdraw of this community once they notice that the teachers cannot really help them. Both scenarios are unfortunate because the kundalini awakens in us a spiritual yearning that most people cannot satisfy completely on their own.

In Buddhism we take refuge to the 'three jewels' before each meditation. These jewels are the Buddha, the teaching and the community of practitioners. So, the community is seen as equally important as the teaching and even as the Buddha himself. What this means is that spiritual development cannot usually be accomplished without spiritual friends who support and encourage us on our way.

I encourage all my kundalini clients to join or re-join a spiritual community of their liking. If they are not part of a group yet, I encourage them to take their time to try as many spiritual and religious groups as possible until they have found one that really suits them.

Other important helpful measures

Most of the following points have already been discussed in chapter three as a preparation for a smooth kundalini awakening. They will also help you once your process throws up some serious trouble. Simply work with the area that you identify as your weakest point and hopefully this will stabilise you. For detailed explanations, please revisit chapter three.

Examine whether you unconsciously have a slightly selfish motivation for awakening the kundalini. Remember that this will always lead to trouble and that the only motivation for a smooth kundalini awakening should be to grow in love and to serve all humankind.

Develop the right amount of willpower – not too lazy and not too pushy and impatient, either.

Develop humility and explore your deeper - sometimes embarrassing and anti-social – motivations and develop some self-deprecating humour.

Make your diet and sleep patterns and entire life-style as healthy as possible.

Pro-actively deal with the conflicts in your primary relationships and make these relationships as loving and honest as possible.

Undo sexual repression (if necessary with the help of a therapist). Do not hesitate to masturbate to release kundalini energy if it feels too overwhelming. (I have had a number of clients who were afraid or unwilling to masturbate and inadvertently aggravated their kundalini symptoms unnecessarily.)

Forgive everyone who has hurt you (without condoning their wrong-doing).

Heal chronic depression, anger, pain and fatigue (if necessary with the help of a therapist).

Let go of any desire for wealth, fame and admiration.

Make your life morally impeccable.

Spend much time in nature, walking, gardening or swimming.

Reduce your workload if you can.

General advice about what to avoid in a kundalini crisis
Both Yvonne Kason's and my own clients have identified a number of things that they found the least helpful in the event of a kundalini crisis or spiritual emergency. The following points are not meant to discourage anyone from seeking help from family members, priests and doctors. It is just intended as a warning that you may not get the help that you are looking for from these people. Unfortunately, there are still very few professionals who are actually qualified to be of real help to someone in the throes of a kundalini crisis.

Talking to family members
Most people without knowledge about the complex symptoms of a kundalini awakening will become afraid and wonder whether you have gone crazy. Your worried family members will often not understand what is going on with you and may also pressurise you to see a doctor or psychiatrist and this will often complicate things even further.

Talking to doctors and psychiatrists
In my experience, there are extremely few doctors or psychiatrists who have even heard about the phenomenon of kundalini, let alone being in a position to offer viable help. They often prescribe drugs meant for mentally ill people that will either not work for you or even aggravate your symptoms even further.

Use of prescription drugs
The widespread use of prescription drugs for depression and anxiety is controversial even for people without kundalini as their effectiveness is questionable and they have plenty of severe side effects. In the case of my kundalini clients, they often make people even worse.

One of my clients was lucky enough to find a retired psychiatrist who had immersed himself in the Hindu religion for many years and was knowledgeable about kundalini problems. He told her outright that kundalini and prescription drugs do not mix well and recommended gentle prayerful meditation, instead. This is exactly my own experience, as well.

The only exception to this rule I would make is in the case of severe insomnia. If you cannot sleep for days in a row, it is important to get some medication to break this negative cycle. I will say more about how to deal with kundalini insomnia later.

Advice from members of traditional religions
I have had numerous clients who experienced a kundalini awakening while on a meditation retreat. They were often dismayed once they realised that their meditation teacher had no idea about kundalini and could not offer any help whatsoever. The same goes for yoga teachers, Christian priests and clerics from all other religions.

The more fundamentalist the cleric, the greater their fear is likely to be of your kundalini symptoms and the more likely it is they will suggest that you may be possessed by devils and demons. Obviously, this will do nothing to alleviate the fears and confusion of someone who has an acute spiritual emergency.

Reading too much about kundalini on the Internet
The Internet can be a useful starting point for finding out about what is going on within you but beyond this basic information it can be a place of great confusion. There are many people who have posted terrible horror stories about kundalini awakening that will frighten even the most confident person.

I strongly advise you not to read these horror stories. Some of them were written by mentally disturbed people who were unaware of the differential diagnosis of mental disease and a kundalini awakening that I will explain later on. Other stories that I have seen were posted by people suffering from sex addiction who wanted to believe that their obsession with degrading sex was something spiritual. Yet other websites about kundalini were written by people who clearly did not know what they were talking about. Generally speaking, the consensus of myself and kundalini experts like Bonnie Greenwell, Yvonne Kason and Phil St. Romain is that kundalini can be challenging but does not have to be a horror trip at all.

Energy healing
In my experience, any form of energy healing like homeopathy, acupuncture, magnet therapy, reiki, lying on of hands, crystal therapy etc. can severely aggravate someone in a kundalini crisis.

I myself tried many of these forms of healing before I knew that I had awakened kundalini and experienced the most dramatic side effects from homeopathy, crystals, reiki and magnet therapy.

My advice is to be very careful and choosy about which healing approach you want to try and to stop immediately you develop unusual symptoms. In my experience, these symptoms do not constitute a healing crisis (things get worse before they get better) as it is commonly assumed by well-meaning practitioners but will simply aggravate your symptoms.

Breathing exercises
I have had a number of clients who have unwittingly created severe negative symptoms for themselves by trying to use all sorts of breathing exercises.

The most prevalent negative symptoms caused by breathing exercises are fear and anxiety. But I have also seen clients who had given themselves heart palpitations through breathing wrongly for an extended amount of time. The common denominator in all forms of debilitating breathing is breathing too fast and too deeply.

By contrast, the most healing form of breathing in a kundalini crisis is the very slow breathing that I have outlined in the anti-anxiety technique. Many people find it hard to believe that this slow breathing will help them because we are taught to 'take a deep breath' in order to calm down. But nothing could be more damaging. Over-breathing is just as detrimental in the long term as over-eating and the key to healthy and anxiety-reducing breathing is to breathe *less*.

I have found that people who are doing breathing exercises are often quite attached to them and are rather unwilling to give them up. It always takes quite a bit of effort from my side to convince them to give slow breathing at least a try. And the moment they try it, the anxiety becomes less within five minutes and is usually gone after 15 minutes. The same is true for the heart palpitations – only it takes days rather than minutes for them to disappear.

Excessive reading of spiritual material
Along with reducing spiritual exercises, it is also important to reduce reading spiritual books. This advice may seem counter-intuitive for someone who is in a spiritual crisis but it is nevertheless true. Reading spiritual material can increase the flow of your kundalini, so it is wise to leave it for a while until your uncomfortable kundalini symptoms have subsided.

Resistance to the kundalini process
The most severe problems during a kundalini awakening are caused through trying to resist this process or by trying to stop it. Some of my clients were outright angry with the person who had awakened the kundalini in them while others were so frightened of the process that they tried not to feel anything below their navel.

Unfortunately, this resistance will severely aggravate all the problems in this process.

Blaming someone else for one's kundalini awakening

I have had a number of clients who blamed others – usually a spiritual teacher – for awakening their kundalini without their consent. This angry attitude always causes terrible suffering.

In order to help yourself in this situation you need to remind yourself that nobody can 'force' anyone to have a kundalini awakening. This process is governed by a deep karmic dynamic and ultimately by our own desire to change and grow. It may be difficult to accept that it was your own (unconscious) desire that brought on your kundalini awakening but in my clinical experience I can see this desire in all of my kundalini clients – those who seek a kundalini awakening consciously, as well as in those to whom it has seemed to happen 'involuntarily'.

The key to coming to terms with this situation is to learn to accept the kundalini process for what it is: the most wonderful opportunity to clear out our unconscious mind and to progress towards enlightenment in the fastest way possible. We also need to learn to forgive the person who we believe has given us a kundalini transmission against our will.

> **Case study: Joyce 41 years**
> Joyce came to see me because she suffered from debilitating kundalini pain and had also experienced a psychosis-like break down. She was extremely angry about having been 'chosen' to endure a kundalini awakening, which she believed had been initiated through the touch (shaktipat) of a spiritual teacher she mistrusted. Yet, Joyce was also very submissive towards this teacher and found it impossible to distance herself from him.
>
> I explained to Joyce that her submissive attitude was unhealthy and that she should say to this teacher (in her mind) that she thought it was wrong that he had given her shaktipat without her consent and that she wanted to part ways with him. Joyce could not muster the courage to do this, despite the fact that she disliked this teacher and did not trust him.
>
> I showed Joyce how to send love to herself and also to this teacher, while simultaneously maintaining her boundaries and letting him float out from her life. I also encouraged Joyce to find a new spiritual community where she could feel more at home.

> After much reluctance, Joyce accepted my approach and started to feel much better. Her physical pain decreased substantially, her psychological confusion disappeared and she found a new home in a spiritual community that suited her much better than her previous one.

Resistance to having to change

As we have discussed at length in chapter two, kundalini 'forces' us to change in virtually every area of our life. Resisting this change can throw up many problems. White Tara advises:

> *You cannot stay the same on your spiritual path and 'simply use' the kundalini bliss to make your existing life more enjoyable. Your self-concept, beliefs, activities and relationships have to become more spiritual in order 'to fit' the bliss of kundalini and if you simply continue in the way you have always done, you will suffer badly. In that way the bliss makes demands on you.*
>
> *Kundalini brings more awareness. But the ego can't cope with more awareness and with too much change. Instead, it arrogantly believes that it is already a 'finished product' and that it can do things alone like an angry toddler. Yet it is this arrogance that brings on most of the negative symptoms of the kundalini awakening.*
>
> *Through your spiritual practice you will sometimes experience many unsettling changes in your personality that 'force' you to change every aspect of your life over and over again. This may bring many losses of old friends, preoccupations and jobs.*
>
> *What's more, with every increase of kundalini your ego-defences are whittled down and new, often-painful aspects of yourself are unleashed from your unconscious mind and must be dealt with.*
>
> *The more you resist these changes the more physical, emotional and spiritual problems you will have on top of the problems that the kundalini has unleashed.*

Yet White Tara also admonishes us to avoid being over-zealous in the process of ego-dissolution. She says:

> *Most of your activities only make sense from the ego-perspective and you will have to let them go. However, you should not force this process of letting go but allow your ego-desires to come to rest naturally because otherwise you will be creating too many negative emotions. This is a gentle process - just like falling asleep.*

Resistance towards amplified emotions and psychological issues

Amplified emotions may be uncomfortable but they are not dangerous. What can cause real problems is our inability to accept our new and more emotional self. This is particularly true for men who believe that 'real men' do not feel fear or cry. These misperceptions will come down with a crash once kundalini is active and it is important to accept and accommodate our new and more emotional sense of self.
It can be deeply humbling to feel more vulnerable and anxious. The more we resist our new emotional self, the more it will hurt. White Tara says:

> *This phase of vulnerability is quite normal and can't be avoided, particularly once you work with kundalini. In fact, this phase is very beneficial because it shows you clearly where you still have work to do. With time, your ability to function without your ego-defences increases as well and you will get less and less stuck in negative emotions.*

So, White Tara is trying to motivate us to stop resisting our feelings of vulnerability and, instead, use them to clear out our negative attitudes and beliefs that led to them in the first place.

Problems relating to the world and ourselves

When kundalini awakens we are changing rapidly and this can lead to problems relating to the world and ourselves in general. As mentioned before, we may become oversensitive, develop powerful emotions where before we could cope perfectly well. We may also find that our relationships do not seem to work anymore and we may even feel a pronounced sense of alienation from the world. Here are a few areas that may become difficult and what you can do about them.

Enlarged depression, anger and fear

I found it very puzzling to find myself in frequent states of acute paranoia and irritation every time I had a new influx of kundalini. I asked White Tara the reason for these amplified emotions and she told me:

> *With fewer ego-defences you become like water that can be penetrated by everything, instead of being like a numb ice-cube. All that may hurt a lot and needs time to integrate and subside.*

Generally speaking, there is no shortcut to getting rid of our amplified emotions. They are not a random aberration of the kundalini process but part of our previously unconscious personality and need to be worked through in detail. It is as if the kundalini is saying to us, 'sort yourself out properly, once and for all!'

The fastest way to dissolve negative emotions is to let them go through the chakra-opening technique that I have explained in chapter four. Basically, as soon as you notice the negative emotion arising in one of your chakras, you relax into the bliss of your kundalini. If you can do this, you do not need any further advice. White Tara puts it like this:

> *Be prepared for a lot of weird negative emotions that were previously unknown. You need to work with these emotions by sending love and flooding the area of the chakra with bliss.*

Given the fact that our emotions are so enlarged during a kundalini process, this simple advice of White Tara may not be enough. Usually, it is necessary to eliminate the negative emotions *gradually* by sending love to yourself and to everyone who is involved in your problem. It may also be necessary to look closely at the negative beliefs that lie at the root of your emotions and investigate your life-story in order to resolve any associated traumas.

Some people who are on the spiritual path scoff at the idea of having to do this kind of psychological work but in my clinical experience with long-term meditation practitioners, this is exactly what they need. Meditation is not the simple short-cut that some people want it to be but needs to be the basis from which we gain self-knowledge rather than greater self-denial and self-repression.

> **Case study Robert, 44 years**
>
> Robert had intensively practised meditation in the Tibetan Buddhist tradition for over 10 years when he came to see me because he was experiencing a major kundalini crisis that manifested itself in frequent temper tantrums and panic attacks. Robert just could not understand why he felt that way because he had been very successful in experiencing bliss and he had had many spiritual visions.
>
> I showed Robert how to send love to himself but he was extremely reluctant. First he argued that 'he' as a person did not exist anyway and that there was no point doing this. I explained to Robert that despite his many spiritual 'achievements', there was still an unenlightened and vulnerable part of him that needed love.
>
> Eventually, Robert agreed to try sending love to himself but when he did he experienced even more anger because loving himself got him in touch with his vulnerabilities – the very thing that he had tried to get away from in his meditation practice. I explained to Robert that he had used his spiritual practice as a means of self-repression and his states of bliss like a drug-trip. What was missing in his approach was the essence of spirituality – love.
>
> After much debate, Robert finally agreed with me and together we embarked on an investigation into why he was so averse to loving himself. It was not long before he unearthed an experience of rejected love in his youth and a traumatic event from his childhood that he had never come to terms with.
>
> I showed Robert how to send love to all the people involved in these painful experiences and also to his vulnerable self he had repressed all these years. It only took a few weeks before Robert's anger and temper tantrums disappeared and he was also able to let go of his anxiety using the anti-anxiety technique.
>
> Subsequently, Robert made the practice of loving-kindness the centrepiece of his meditation practice and from then on his kundalini problems were greatly diminished.

Apart from sending love and relaxing the emotions in our body-mind, it can also be helpful to keep the focus on our navel when we are engulfed in major storms of negative emotions. This is how White Tara explained it to me:

> *Keeping the focus on the navel has generally a stabilising effect and you will become more imperturbable. If there is too much energy in the higher chakras, you will become more unstable.*

Another important measure for stabilising yourself in times of high emotions is to adopt a very straight body posture. Particularly, if you are experiencing floods of tears, you can help yourself by maintaining this posture. Cry with your eyes open, head up and back erect. I promise you that your tears will subside within less than five minutes.

Generally speaking, never allow yourself to act out your negative emotions by pounding a pillow in anger or screaming and shouting. While doing this may bring relief in the short term, it will only aggravate your emotions in the long run. It is much better to simply observe the emotions and to work with the anti-anxiety technique and relaxation technique we discussed earlier.

Summary of dealing with strong emotions
Notice the arising negative emotion in a particular chakra and dissolve this energy into the bliss of your kundalini.
If this is too difficult, send love to yourself and everyone who is involved in your problem.
Relax the chakra in which you feel the negative emotions with a suitable visualisation.
Use the anti-anxiety technique for fear and panic.
Maintain a very straight body posture for floods of tears.
Focus your attention on your navel in the case of particularly overwhelming emotions.
Never allow yourself to act out your negative emotions.
Analyse the attitudes and beliefs underlying your emotions and change as necessary.

Oversensitivity
As we have discussed before, Kundalini can make us much more sensitive. Activities that we have enjoyed before may become unbearable and we may not be able to cope where we have coped perfectly well before.

I myself certainly had a problem understanding and accepting this. I still wanted to go to a restaurant or to a cinema and could not understand why I suddenly found the level of noise intolerable. Worst of all was my inability to even enjoy my beloved country walks. I just did not want to accept this and tried doing these things over and over again only to find myself a self-doubting bundle of nerves unable to understand what was going on within me. White Tara told me:

People think that they will become tougher and tougher on the spiritual path but that is not true. All good spiritual practice makes you happier on the one hand but exposes your weaknesses simultaneously. This is because spiritual practice takes your ego-defences away.

Your ego-defences are like a set of tensions. Without your ego-defences you become softer and more vulnerable and can be touched and penetrated by everything. If you are not yet stable in your practice, you will often overreact to the smallest things. This can hurt a lot and intense pain and intense bliss will alternate.

If you can experience strong bliss, you will experience small disturbances as major issues, including noise, ugliness and the suffering of others. This is much like the way a black spot appears even blacker on a white screen than on a dark grey screen. This can greatly upset you.

And White Tara gave me these pieces of succinct advice:

The navel practice makes you much tougher and more able to endure suffering.

Bliss-practice must always be combined with loving-kindness. Love will lessen all sorts of negative symptoms. You should put bubbles of love around yourself and others.

You may need to retreat into the house and give up all sorts of activities that increase your symptoms. Most of all, you need patience with these symptoms. They will subside as you get better used to your new and more blissful sense of self.

I really did not like the advice of having to retreat into the house, particularly as my oversensitivity went on for several years and at times I felt almost crippled by my noise intolerance. However, over the years this problem has greatly improved thanks to White Tara's suggestions of retreating, sending love and navel practice. It has worked well and for the last few years my noise oversensitivity has hardly bothered me at all. My nerves have become more robust and I also have changed my life in so many ways that I simply do not encounter this problem very often anymore.

Confrontation with our shadow side
For some people it can be a terrible shock to discover darker and even outright nasty impulses within themselves and others during a kundalini awakening. For example, one of my male clients confided in me with great distress that on his last visit to his brother he had had vivid 'memories' that he had sexually abused his young nieces in his last life. He was greatly relieved to hear that these kinds of impressions or 'memories' are normal during a kundalini awakening and that the best way of dealing with them is to see them as belonging to the collective unconscious that Carl Jung proposed. I advised my client to counteract these impressions by visualising his nieces enveloped in bubbles of divine love. He felt better almost immediately.

The more self-righteous and convinced we are of our 'goodness', 'innocence' and 'positive intentions', the more upsetting these kinds of discoveries will be. For people who have a fundamentalist outlook on life and divide everyone into either 'completely good' or 'completely bad', this can precipitate a major crisis. They may even believe that they are possessed by the devil when in reality they have only discovered their shadow side. White Tara explains:

> *You may be able to see many negative things in yourself and others that you didn't see before. This is because more life force means more awareness. For example, you may start to see the many forms of selfishness, stupidity and envy in yourself and others. This can be quite shocking and saddening.*

In order to understand this dynamic it helps to imagine our mind as being like an iceberg. The top of the iceberg sticking out of the water is your conscious mind and the much larger piece of ice under the water is your unconscious mind. Kundalini will make this unconscious mind conscious in a gradual or abrupt way and you need to be prepared to find some negative and even nasty impulses. This can be rather embarrassing but not dangerous. On the contrary, knowing about these destructive attitudes will enable you to manage them rather to act them out in an unconscious way.

The key here is to love and accept ourselves *with* all our weaknesses and negative impulses and yet never to act them out. This attitude will make us more humble, less judgemental and much more compassionate towards the shortcomings of others, too. It is the hallmark of a truly evolved person that they know they are capable of every atrocity, yet have perfect self-control.

Emanuel Swedenborg, the great Swedish mystic of the 18th century expressed this dynamic in the following way: He taught that everybody has the entire heaven and the entire hell within their own mind. Our task, he said, is to *choose* to stay in heaven from moment to moment and to be wary of the temptation of hell *forever*.

I could not agree more and frequently use Swedenborg's metaphor when teaching my students. It is the very idea of trying to be a *completely* good person who does not have a shadow side that creates so much damage. As soon as we develop the humble view of seeing all our potential darkness, the world is already a safer place.

In Tibetan Buddhism this dynamic is explained with the idea that we have lived millions of lives and that we have committed every possible atrocity. We are reassured by our Buddhist teachers that there is no need whatsoever to feel guilty if some of these 'past-life memories' come up and simply have compassion with ourselves and carry on as usual with our spiritual practice.

Sense of alienation from the world

A kundalini awakening can spark experiences of pronounced alienation from the world that can be confusing and upsetting.

I remember one day when I collected my young son from his football practice session and went with him to a small playground nearby. I felt the usual ecstasy and bliss coursing through my mind and body but I was also acutely aware that I was totally out of sync with the other mums who were also there on the playground. I felt I had nothing in common with them and their approach to life. I also found the little pieces of litter on the playground very disgusting and was confused that nobody else seemed to mind. I became frightened by my thoughts and feelings and wondered whether there was something deeply wrong with me as I felt so alienated and unable to connect with others. White Tara comforted me like this:

> *When kundalini is flowing you may lose interest in people and activities that you have enjoyed before and find little things very disturbing. This can be very upsetting because you do not yet have the positive relationships that match your new state of mind.*

As I have already told you, I have found a way of connecting with people through my work that is very satisfying to me. But I also know from my clients that some of them feel profoundly alone with their new experiences. However, in order to overcome these feelings of alienation, it is important to make an effort to find new friends. These new friends are most likely to be found in places like spiritual centres.

At our workplace we may feel alienated too and it can be difficult to make changes because we may be tied to our old workplace due to financial responsibilities or other practicalities. Even if we are able to make a career change to a more satisfying career, we may not be able to attract clients and customers to make this a success. In White Tara's words:

> *When you have lots of kundalini you have a lot more to give but not always the karmic connections to do so. This can lead to much frustration.*

White Tara explained to me that this sense of alienation from the world is due to an imbalance in our chakra system. She said:

> *If there is an imbalance between an open heart and head chakra on the one side and a closed navel on the other, you can experience great bliss in the meditation but you will not be able to manifest this divine experience in tangible relationships and material surroundings.*

And she gave me this advice:

> *You need to strengthen your navel chakra by focusing on it so that you have more power to change and create your personal universe to suit your changing needs.*

> *You can be reassured that your inability to enjoy the outside world is only temporary and that once you have developed enough kundalini, it will only be a matter of time before your divine mandala manifests.*

I would not say that I have manifested a 'divine mandala' but I certainly have come a long way from the time that I felt so alienated from the world. The more kundalini we develop through the navel practice, the easier it will be to change our life and manifest our dreams. Doing so is not some magic trick but simply requires determined and persistent work to create a life that is good for others and ourselves.

It goes without saying that all our wishes should be beneficial not only for ourselves but for others too, as otherwise our kundalini awakening will derail into a giant ego-trip. How to do this well is explained in my book 'Advanced Manifesting – Tibetan Buddhist Secrets for Manifesting Your Dreams'. White Tara also gave me this important piece of advice:

> *If you grieve about your loss of enjoyment of the world, you need to remind yourself that the outside world, for example nature, cannot be enjoyed as such. If you disconnect from your divine essence even the most beautiful surroundings cannot make you happy. You can only be happy if you are in touch with your divine essence, which then radiates out and manifests in an inspiring surrounding. In other words, a beautiful sight is like an adornment of your inner beautiful self.*

Energy problems

During a voluntary kundalini process we should try to accumulate as much energy as possible and balance this energy with an equal amount of love. But this energy accumulation process can lead to various energy problems and therefore we have to proceed carefully and with caution. White Tara warns:

> *The great energy of the kundalini is not always easy to bear. It can be tiring to the body - just like physical exercise. You have to train yourself to tolerate it more and more. If you have too much energy, you may want to jump up and down to get rid of this over-excitement but the point is to learn to let it build up increasingly in your body, while staying outwardly serene.*

When talking about energy problems, we need to remember that White Tara has taught us that energy is not a 'thing' that exists in and of itself but rather arises from some sort of friction between our own conflicting impulses. Therefore, no matter how much it feels like some 'real energy' is moving inside us, we are simply feeling our own conflicting impulses that have manifested in that way. The main conflict that we all experience is in finding the right balance between love and power.

The same is true for so-called 'energy blocks'. I had numerous experiences of feeling that the energy 'got stuck' at various places in my body. In reality, I had simply tensed up in these places due to the conflicts they represented. For example, for several years, on and off, I experienced a 'block' in my heart chakra. If I had maintained a faulty materialistic view I might have tried to 'push' the energy away in some way. But the real solution was to look at my fears around the topic of love and to practice loving-kindness in order for this 'block' to disappear. I work in this way with all of my kundalini clients too and we usually succeed together in dissolving these 'blocks' by using this approach.

As we have discussed before, the more we try to resist the kundalini process and the more we try to manipulate 'the energy', the more it will hurt. So, the general advice here is to relax, to love ourselves, and to become more aware of our inner conflicting impulses, instead of trying to 'push and pull at the energy'.

Fear of feeling energy moving inside us

A number of my clients feel fear about their energy phenomena. As we have discussed before, the energy may be experienced as heat or like crawling ants or as a tingling. Another kundalini sign is 'wandering symptoms', for example pain, sadness or anxiety that wanders from one part of the body to another. The anxious questions that I hear over and over again are, 'is this normal?' and 'will this harm my body?'.

My answer is that during a kundalini awakening the unusual is normal. Kundalini phenomena may be weird, they may be frightening and uncomfortable but they are *not* dangerous. I have yet to see anyone who has been harmed physically or psychologically by the kundalini. The kundalini in itself is never the problem – it simply presents us with a magnified version of ourselves. The real problem comes from our fear and our resistance to this phenomenon.

In our fear, we may associate all sorts of frightening ideas with our kundalini symptoms. We may be afraid that we are going mad, that the devil is influencing us, or that some day we will 'explode' from all this energy. But none of this is true. Kundalini energy coursing around our body is no more dangerous than sexual energy coursing around our abdomen or hot flushes rising up our body during menopause. All these phenomena can be overwhelmingly strong and really uncomfortable but they are definitely not dangerous. It is our frightened and unfounded associations with these phenomena that are the problem and never the kundalini in itself.

> **Case study, Joanne, 33 years**
> The most extreme example of fear of kundalini symptoms is a woman I knew many years ago before I became a kundalini therapist so, sadly, I was not in a position to help her. This woman felt the kundalini rising up her spine and into her head and she was convinced that if she went to sleep, the energy would rise out of her crown chakra and she would die. So, she kept herself awake for weeks at a time until she completely broke down and had to go into a psychiatric hospital. The only thing the psychiatrists did was giving her strong sleeping pills and, obviously, she did not die when she finally fell asleep. Her sanity was restored within one or two days but she went through this cycle a number of times because she had noone who could reassure her.

The solution to fear about energy phenomena is to become informed about kundalini and to stop buying into irrational beliefs the way Joanne did. You should also avoid reading any horror stories on the Internet from people who, unfortunately, will try to convince you that kundalini is really dangerous.

In the next step, you need to learn to reduce your fear using the anti-anxiety technique that I outlined previously. If this is not enough, it is important to find an experienced guide who you can trust and who will help you to reduce your anxiety.

Energetic overload

Many people experience phases of energetic overload during their kundalini process. But before we go more deeply into the topic, remember that the term 'energetic overload' is just a manner of speaking. There is no real overloaded energy but simply places in our body-mind in which our inner conflicts become so pressing that they crystallise into pain and uncomfortable feelings. White Tara says:

> *If you focus on bliss and kundalini for too long, you may experience an energetic overload. More energy is not simply better. You need to have as much energy as is suitable for your system. Too much and all of your physical and emotional issues increase massively, like strong anger, anxiety and confusion.*

How do we recognise energetic overload? The first sign of this difficult phenomenon is that your emotions feel like physical pain, for example, depression may feel like a pain in the chest. The second sign of energetic overload is that your emotional and physical pain becomes *worse* during chakra work, rather than better. For example, you may do all the things you have learnt in chapter four, like smiling with love into a chakra and seeing it open like a beautiful flower for half an hour in full concentration. But instead of relaxation and bliss, you experience more and more pain in the chakra. That is what we call energetic overload.

If you suffer in this way, you first need to rule out any physical illness by getting a proper health-check with a professional. Sometimes the kundalini can mimic physical disease in an uncanny way. You may remember that I had the textbook symptoms of gallbladder disease but that the ultrasound check found that my gallbladder was in perfect condition.

Sometimes we are dealing with a proper disease and it is very important not to miss it by assigning all our aches and pains to our kundalini process. One of my clients suffered from confusion and frequent vomiting and was convinced that these were kundalini symptoms. I urged him to get checked out and the doctor found that he was suffering from a rare, serious illness that needed urgent medication. Luckily the treatment for this illness was easy and straightforward and my client was soon feeling better.

What can we do in the case of an energetic overload? White Tara gives us this general advice:

> *The real reason for energetic overload is lack of love, which would spread the energy out. This problem can be remedied by practising loving-kindness.*

It cannot be overstated how important the focus on loving-kindness is during a kundalini awakening. It literally should be the foundation of all our practices. You may remember from chapter one that enlightenment is the perfect balance of the sea of love and life force/kundalini. So, it is self-evident that we can correct an energetic overload by focusing more on love.

Aside from loving-kindness practices, here are a few more tips on how to reduce the symptoms of energetic overload. First of all, always remember to visualise your body as hollow, filled with brilliant light and deeply relax the overloaded area with any method that works for you. In chapter four I explained the visualisation of an opening flower and light emerging from the open flower spreading out to the ends of the universe. You can try to use this visualisation and see if it helps.

Another thing you can try for energy overload is massage. Vigorously rub, knock and knead the area of the energetic overload or use an electrical massager. Do this vigorous massage for a few seconds and then move the hand away from the affected area in a graceful movement to let the energy disperse. Alternatively, try to stretch the affected area by bending forwards, backwards and sideways. Try to tune into the natural bliss of the chakra and notice whether this brings relief. If yes, repeat frequently, until the energetic overload has dispersed.

If none of these measures work, you need to shift your attention away from the energetically overloaded chakra by focusing on another chakra. Energy follows thought and therefore it is important to avoid giving the overloaded chakra any more attention. Avoid feeling 'into the chakra' or even thinking about the chakra because this will only increase the energetic overload. Instead, do not give any attention to this chakra at all for a few days or even some weeks. White Tara gave me this advice:

> *If concentrating on a chakra increases a feeling of bloating or pain, concentrate on the chakra above it or below it, whatever works best. Or focus on the navel to draw excess energy into it because the navel chakra can store more energy than the other chakras. Also, make sure you focus more on your spine and not on the front of the body.*

The problem of energy overload can particularly affect the heart or the top of the head (the crown chakra in the Hindu system) resulting in heart pain and head pressure. That is why I have advised you to focus mostly on your forehead rather than on your crown during your daily meditation practice.

If you feel heart pain that you cannot disperse, you can try to imagine a feeling of love and compassion in the palms of your hands or in your eyes when you do your loving-kindness meditation. Also, increase the time you spend focusing on the navel in order to stop these problems occurring in the first place. White Tara told me:

> *The safest place to store your increased energy is your navel. Therefore, the more kundalini you have, the more you should focus on your navel in order to store this energy safely. If you do not keep the energy in the navel, it will just amplify what is going on in your mind and higher chakras, which is not always a good thing. You need to keep the focus on the navel because this will stabilise you.*

In practice, this means that sometimes we need to stop focusing on a certain chakra for days or even weeks at a time until the energy overload has dispersed naturally. Instead, we should focus on one of the other chakras, on our hands, eyes and on the navel. You need to experiment to see what works best.

Energetic overload in certain chakras does not happen by accident. The chakra involved always represents a topic that we have not resolved within ourselves. It therefore important to investigate the 'topic of the chakra' and to explore what makes it difficult to experience it in a more positive way.

For example, when the energetic overload happens in the head we need to investigate questions about how self-aware we want to be and whether we are in denial about some part of ourselves. If the overload is in the heart, we should investigate any fears and vulnerabilities around the topic of love and emotional support. Please revisit chapter four to look at the different themes connected with each chakra.

Summary of how to remedy an energetic overload:
Get checked out by a doctor to rule out any physical disease.
Focus more on loving-kindness during your daily meditation.
Visualise your body as hollow and filled with brilliant light.
Relax the area of the energy overload deeply by using a visualisation of an opening flower as described in chapter four.
Use vigorous massage and stretching exercises to disperse the energetic overload.
If the relaxation and massage do not work, avoid focusing on the associated chakra for several days or weeks until the overload subsides.
Instead, focus on a chakra above or below the affected chakra, on your navel, your hands, your eyes and your spine.
Investigate the topic of the associated chakra and rectify any faulty beliefs and fears around this topic.

Too little energy
Another problem we may encounter is energy deficiency. This often manifests in feelings of sadness, depression, listlessness or fatigue. White Tara says:

> *Some problems in the chakras are caused by too little energy, for example, depressive feelings in the head. If that happens, you need to focus more on another chakra, for example the navel until the energy is strong enough to supply the necessary energy for this chakra. You simply need to try out which chakra is remedying the problem.*

Generally speaking, fatigue and lack of energy is caused by an over-focus on the upper chakras. This can easily happen by meditating for too long on formless meditation or calming meditations like observing the breath. I myself struggled for years with some form of peculiar depression that seemed to be aggravated by the simple breath meditation that I did at the time. Not knowing what caused my problem, I tried to cure it by meditating more, which only made my problem worse. It was only when I focused more on the blissful energy of the kundalini that I was able to remedy this problem.

Another cause of lack of energy is having an aversion to the powerful energy of the lower chakras. There are many people who follow a spiritual path and repress their sexual, angry and powerful sides in a misguided attempt to become more 'spiritually advanced'. Unfortunately, this approach rarely works and these people frequently find themselves plagued by tiredness and sickliness. The problem is that by repressing our power and also our anger we often lose our vitality, as well. Admittedly, anger is a tricky emotion because it can be destructive but repression is not the answer.

In Tibetan Buddhism, we are taught that within a 'small anger' there is the gift of discriminating wisdom, which means that through a small amount of anger we become able to see things more clearly. Therefore, symptoms of low energy can often be remedied by showing a person how to deal with their anger more skilfully and embrace their own power. The following case-study shows how this may look in practice.

Case study: Adrian, 46 years

Adrian is a lovely and very softly spoken man who came to see me because he suffered from debilitating fatigue and some aches and pains after a kundalini awakening. Adrian spent several hours a day in meditation but was too weak to hold down a job.

It was clear to me just by listening to Adrian's voice that he was severely out of touch with the more powerful energy of his lower chakras. After thinking about it for a little while, I advised him to stop meditating for the time being and instead to take up a martial art and to imagine that he was an angry person.

Adrian followed my advice and after only two weeks his fatigue was more than half gone and he was able to work whole days and his sex drive returned, as well. Adrian was very pleased about this development but also rather confused why things as 'mundane' as anger and martial arts were helping him. I explained to

> Adrian that he had over-focused on his top three chakras and neglected the more masculine energy in his lower chakras. Adrian understood my approach but he was rather anxious that he would become too angry. I then showed Adrian how to work with his navel chakra without getting angry and soon his fatigue was gone for good.

Insomnia

A large percentage of my kundalini clients suffer from pronounced insomnia with some of them not sleeping at all for days at a time. This insomnia aggravates every challenge throughout the day and, if it goes on for long enough, it can lead to hallucinations and fears of going crazy.

In my clinical experience, the kundalini makes it more likely that we experience insomnia but the actual trigger is our inner unresolved conflicts. The most typical of these inner conflicts is anger that we cannot own up to, for example towards family members or children. And the solution is to own up to the anger and find a creative compromise for the underlying conflict.

Unfortunately, prolonged insomnia creates a vicious cycle because the longer it lasts, the more tensions and anxiety are created, which make it even harder to get back to sleep naturally. It is for this reason that I recommend taking medication and even prescription drugs for insomnia. Here is some general advice for treating and avoiding insomnia:

Approach for insomnia

Stop all practices that create more kundalini. Focus purely on loving yourself and others and also on relaxation exercises.
Look deeply into any reasons that may create anger and resentment in you (even very mildly). Practice forgiveness and try to find practical solutions to the relationships that are making you angry.
Search your mind deeply for any inner conflict you may have and try to address the issues.
Cut out all caffeine.
Stop all strenuous intellectual activity from late afternoon onwards.
When going to bed, use the sleep meditation outlined below.

I have used the following sleep meditation myself and I have also taught it to all my insomniac clients with good results. I have found that doing this sleep meditation throughout the night is almost as good as real sleep. You can do it for hours and hours and in the morning you will 'wake up' feeling almost as good as if you had slept properly.

> **Exercise: Sleep meditation**
> **Lie down** in your favourite sleep position and imagine that you are lying in the arms of your very large higher power. You are safe and loved like a baby.
> **Remind yourself** that you do not need to sleep as long as you do this sleep meditation.
> **Relax all tensions** everywhere in your body. Simply imagine that all tensions dissolve like mist in the morning sun or into a liquid mash.
> **Imagine** that your entire brain dissolves into a liquid mash. Drop you jaw slightly while imagining this.
> **Let all** arising thoughts and feelings melt away with your dissolving brain.
> **Keep relaxing** your body, brain and thoughts in this way.
> **At some point**, you will notice dream images emerging from your unconscious mind. This is a very good sign as you have successfully changed your brain waves to sleep mode even while you are still awake. Simply continue doing your sleep meditation and remind yourself that you do not need to sleep 'properly'.
> **When you are** at the very verge of falling sleep you may notice a small amount of fear in the heart. Be pleased with yourself that you were able to come so far and simply relax this fear, as well.
> **Most importantly**, keep reminding yourself that you do not need to sleep and that doing this meditation is good enough.

Attachment to bliss

It is easy to understand how attachment to kundalini bliss develops. Once the bliss is flowing, it seems like a whole new and wonderful world has opened up. It is natural to become rather attached to this newfound bliss, which is why I have already written about this danger in chapter four. The main danger of attachment to bliss is ego-inflation and rebound anger and depression.

The people who are most at risk of developing attachment to bliss are meditation students who have been successful in awakening the kundalini. They then embark on some sort of honeymoon with their new-found ecstasy and the more they believe that their bliss will last forever, the bigger the crash will be once their unconscious mind opens up and releases difficult unconscious material. If they then attempt to repress this material, it can develop into an even bigger crisis. White Tara warns:

> *If you repress the material that has been unleashed from your unconscious mind through the kundalini process, it can lead to psychosomatic symptoms. You should be very careful about this point.*

What distinguishes attachment to bliss from simply enjoying this experience? Attachment is characterised by a certain rigidity, by holding on to this experience and by being inflexible. By contrast, a healthy relationship with the bliss is characterised by enjoying it while it lasts yet being willing to give it up in order to attend to the needs of others. Non-attachment to bliss means realising that the core of all spiritual development is love and not bliss.

Therefore, we should always keep in mind the need to use our experience of bliss to develop more love and wisdom and not just enjoy it for its own sake like a drug-trip. Developing wisdom means using the experience of bliss to explore and stabilise the experience of non-self that we discussed in chapter four and will be exploring further in chapter seven. By contrast, people who try to 'own' the bliss and use it as something that makes them special are completely missing the point.

It is important to be willing to give up the bliss and whole-heartedly attend to any problem that arises from our unconscious mind. Noone is immune from these challenges and any attitude of 'not needing to deal with our psychological problems anymore' will lead to serious trouble. Remember, our psychological issues often become aggravated during a kundalini awakening and we need to be ready to explore and rectify the irrational beliefs, old resentments and childhood traumas that trigger them.

We need also to be willing to give up our bliss if the needs of the people around us require attention. In a family, for example, we need to attend to a cranky child or an unhappy spouse without blaming them for disturbing our ecstasy. If we are unwilling to do this, we have developed an unhealthy attachment to bliss. Unfortunately, I have witnessed on several occasions how a family father withdrew from his wife and children to attend to his 'spiritual work' but in reality neglected his responsibilities to them. It sometimes takes a bit of organisation to carve out some meditation times in a hectic family and work situation but, being a mother and wife myself, I know it can be done if we really want to achieve this.

Rebound depression or anger

A big problem resulting from attachment to bliss is rebound depression and anger. As I have mentioned before, these feelings are an almost unavoidable by-product of strong experiences of bliss and ecstasy. I myself have noticed this anger frequently when I have entered the hustle and bustle of family life after a particularly blissful meditation session. Small irritations seem to grow out of proportion and lead to strong anger. This problem can become even more pronounced if we have been meditating for an extended period of time in a meditation retreat. We may also experience a pronounced depressive response. White Tara says:

> *You may experience a sharp contrast between exalted states in the meditation sessions and being unstable and negative in daily life.*
>
> *The happier you are in the meditation, the more impatient and even angry you may become with the inevitable irritations of daily life because they seem to pull you down from your exalted state.*

A first step to overcoming rebound anger and depression is to know about these problems in advance so as not to be caught unaware. We can then make the transition from meditation to daily life more consciously and be better prepared to let go of any anger or depression as these feelings arise. We need also to resolve to put love before bliss so that we are ready to help anyone who needs attention, even if this means that we will lose our bliss in the process.

If you feel depressed after a blissful meditation retreat, it is important not to give into these depressive feelings but to keep practicing in daily life. The harder the transition from the retreat to your daily life, the more you need to practice while going about your daily activities. White Tara gives us this advice:

> *The split between bliss in meditation and instability outside meditation is quite normal and even advanced masters experience it. You set yourself up for frustration if you expect that you can maintain the bliss in daily life too soon.*
>
> *You need to be patient with this problem – the solution cannot be hurried. You need to prepare yourself for possible frustration, particularly after an*

intensely blissful meditation experience.

It is also important that we are ready to change our life to accommodate our new and more blissful self. For example, we may not be able to do certain types of stressful and spiritually meaningless work anymore. So, in order to avoid constant rebound anger, we may have to change our job. The same may be true for all relationships with people who do not strive to develop themselves.

I myself had to learn these lessons and I admit that it is not always easy to give up the attachments to certain people or activities that we have out-grown but still crave. Once we can let go, we will feel all the better for it.

Attachment to the sea of love

Some people become attached to the experience of the sea of love, which is a sense of utter stillness and void. White Tara says about this phenomenon:

> *Some people are attached to the sea of love and inner peace. This is a form of spiritual laziness.*

Attachment to the sea of love always goes together with an over-focus on the upper chakras and, as we have discussed before, this can lead to fatigue, listlessness and sometimes chronic pain. The 19th century occultist Dion Fortune talks about such people as 'sickly mystics' who drained energy from the more powerful people in her magic circles. Dion's description is a bit disparaging but explains quite well what this condition looks like.

The remedy is, obviously, to let go of this one-sided focus and to channel our spiritual endeavours more strongly into raising our kundalini and into more active forms of helping others. We must never forget that the ultimate state is the perfect balance between love and power, between stillness and energy and between upper and lower chakras. Every time we lose this perfect balance, we need to remedy it by focusing more strongly on the opposite pole.

Ego-inflation

The biggest danger caused by attachment to bliss is that our ego becomes filled with pride about our 'superiority' and we lose our compassion for others who are still struggling. In the worst-case scenario, we may even develop delusions of grandeur. White Tara warns:

> *A major pitfall on the spiritual path is becoming over-confident through all sorts of worldly and spiritual success. Your ego may become arrogant, complacent and start 'pushing its luck'. You may also feel entitled to dominate other people. All this will bring repercussions and suffering. With an over-confident mindset, you may also think wrongly that you do not need a teacher anymore.*

Every kundalini awakening will bring our unconscious issues to the foreground and if we have repressed feelings of entitlement and grandeur, they will certainly come up in time. If we then allow these feelings to go unchecked, they will lead to much suffering. The more attachment to bliss and our imagined superiority we have, the bigger this crisis will be.

I have seen this problem within myself and also in fellow meditation students who I met on retreats and on Internet-based kundalini forums. Here is just one example: On one forum, a woman called Tina explained that she had her own kundalini awakening a year before and that she was now at a point of being able to give shaktipat to others (transmission of kundalini by touch). She then went on to describe how she had facilitated a kundalini awakening in a friend of hers. However, from Tina's description I strongly suspected that her friend did not have a kundalini awakening but rather the onset of a major mental crisis. The mother of her friend was in a state of high anxiety about her daughter but Tina treated her worries with mild contempt. This is a typical example of a kundalini awakening derailing into an ego-trip. Instead of giving up the idea that she had given shaktipat and supporting the distressed sister of her friend, this woman was only concerned about her own 'amazing abilities' and wanted to get confirmation about them from the forum members.

In order to avoid going on such an ego-trip, you should be on the lookout for self-righteous anger, ideas of entitlement and megalomaniac ideas. Reject all these impulses and instead focus on loving-kindness and the experience of non-self that we have discussed in chapter four.

Another form of ego inflation is the belief that one is beyond things that ordinary people need - like relationships, food or spiritual practice. This is something Gopi Krishna describes in his books quite vividly. Every time he had a fresh influx of kundalini, he had the strong impulse that he did not need food anymore and nearly starved himself to death on several occasions. He also wanted to leave his home and wife and become a wandering hermit without any possessions.

In my work, I have also seen a number of kundalini clients who believed that they could exist without loving relationships and survive 'on their kundalini bliss alone', so to speak.

The reality is that kundalini will make us less dependent on many things and relationships but not completely independent. It will become easier, for example, to give up addictive habits, meaningless entertainment and dysfunctional relationships. However, it would be a vast exaggeration to believe that we can become completely free of the need for food or loving relationships. All our basic human needs will continue and we will get ourselves into trouble if, in our initial kundalini euphoria, we believe that we can do without them.

Generally speaking, feelings of superiority are less common among my clients because these people have already developed a crisis that has erased most feelings of grandeur. Instead, a healthy sense of humility has set in that motivated them to ask a kundalini therapist for help. White Tara gives us these tips to remedy any tendency towards ego-inflation:

> *Scrutinise yourself daily and thoroughly. Apologise if necessary. Always be on the lookout for arrogance and lack of love. Send love to all difficult people daily. Be humble in all conversations. Avoid talking positively about yourself because it creates envy and anger. Never try to progress without first forming a deeply loving relationship with your guru and deity.*
>
> *With kundalini all your wishes will have more power and this can lead to powerful resistance from other people. For that reason, you need to make doubly sure to make your wishes with love, always and everywhere.*

The remedy for attachment to bliss:

Thoroughly understand the danger of a kundalini awakening leading to an ego-trip.
Be prepared for rebound anger and depression and be especially aware during the transition between meditation and daily life.
Always be ready to give up your bliss if emerging material from your unconscious mind demands your attention or when other people need your help.
Monitor yourself critically and reject all prideful self-perception or any ideas of complete independence.
Take ample time to meditate on loving-kindness daily.
Focus on the experience of non-self that we discussed in chapter four.
Closely connect to a spiritual teacher who will confront you with your errors.

Difficulty tolerating bliss - the happiness ceiling

It may sound difficult to believe but it can actually be difficult to tolerate bliss and ecstasy. I have observed all these factors both in others and myself and White Tara told me why this might happen. Here is what she said:

> The happiness ceiling is the inability to tolerate happiness and positive events. When you get 'too happy' the ego becomes afraid of being superfluous, bored and even destroyed. The ego thrives on problems to be solved and on goals to be achieved. When you are too happy, there are neither problems nor unachieved goals. So, instead of focusing on helping others, the ego starts to invent some new personal problems.
>
> If you feel unconsciously guilty for having done bad things in the past, you cannot allow yourself to feel real happiness or a sense of fulfilment when the opportunity comes along.
>
> More happiness can lead to anxiety because it is unfamiliar, unknown and feels very fragile – as if it can be lost any moment. The old misery feels much more solid and reliable. In order to get back to familiar ground, your mind will start to 'invent' a problem.
>
> The happiness ceiling can also be caused through fear of not being deserving, fear of envy from others and fear of causing pain to others by upstaging them. Also, feeling all this pleasure can feel rather indulgent and evoke resistance from your repressive side.

And she gives us this advice:

> The most general solution to the happiness ceiling is to relate to the world and yourself with more love, with gratefulness and by uniting with what is wonderful.
>
> Feeling bliss is not indulgent because it will cleanse you from all your residual negative emotions. You should practice in this way as much as possible.
>
> You need to learn to trust that perfect happiness is possible. The Buddhist

truth that 'life is suffering' is only true if you seek happiness from outside sources. But if you rely on your kundalini bliss, life is a continuous flow of happiness.

When you are very happy about something, don't try to 'milk' the situation for happiness because this will make you believe that this happiness comes from the outside situation. Then fear will arise that your happiness can be taken away from you. Instead, continue to rely on inner bliss and focus on helping others.

Finally, White Tara gives us this really important piece of advice:

Focus on negativity and problems disappearing from your life rather than on trying to get to higher and higher amounts of bliss.

This last piece of advice is important because it counteracts any tendency to use the bliss like a drug. Instead, we should be using it for healing and rectifying our faults and problems. After all, what really matters is that we become of real benefit to others and not that we have the most extreme states of bliss.

Difficulty in dealing with the paranormal

Everyone who has a kundalini awakening will have paranormal experiences sooner or later. The better we are prepared for these experiences, the less frightening and confusing they will be.

There are positive and enjoyable paranormal experiences and negative and frightening ones. Whether a paranormal experience is positive needs to be ascertained by its effects and not only by how enjoyable and impressive it is. If we have a beautiful vision of the divine, for example, we need to pay close attention to how this vision makes us feel once it is over. If we feel more humble and loving, it is a positive vision. But if this experience leaves us with a feeling of pride or a sense of being chosen, we need to regard the experience as an ego-trip.

In order to deal with frightening experiences of the paranormal, we need to understand that in the world of the paranormal our usual subject-object division ('I' am here and 'you' are over there) is not true anymore. If we have a vision of a horrible demon, for example, this demon is a product of our own unconscious mind while also existing from its own side.

Generally speaking, the more we believe that a phenomenon exists from its own side and the more attention we give to it, the more our belief will appear to be true. In other words, by giving attention to something paranormal we are feeding and nurturing these experiences and they will become more and more real and finally appear as adopting a life of their own. If we understand this dynamic, it is clear that the best way to deal with frightening paranormal experiences is to give them as little attention as possible.

You may wonder at this point whether positive experiences like visions of a divine being or indeed the readings in this book are merely figments of the imagination. White Tara told me this:

> *Positive experiences are positive because they are real. Everything positive is real and everything negative is unreal. Every form of suffering arises from your fears and angers and you know that these are just distortions of your life force. But positive experiences are real because they come from your divine essence. In that sense, you can say that divine beings come from your mind, too. But as you know, the divine essence is the same in all beings. So, in that sense, you can see that divine beings arise from your mind and also exist from their own side.*
>
> *The subject-object division is an illusion for negative things, as well as for positive experiences. But what distinguishes those two is whether they are real or not. And only the positive experiences are real.*

So, White Tara is saying that our sense of self and the self of our higher power are interconnected but this does not mean that our higher power is unreal. By contrast, everything negative that emerges from our mind, whether it manifests in negative emotions or in 'demons' surrounding us, is not real and needs to be ignored.

I realise that this advice may not always be easy to put into practice because the kundalini makes all our thoughts and feelings appear more vivid and that can sometimes be very frightening. Therefore, we need to keep firmly in our mind that even if these experiences appear as very real, they are still only a product of our own unconscious mind and are essentially harmless - just like a frightening dream.

If your paranormal experiences are so frightening that you cannot ignore them anymore, try to fix your mind on your higher power to the exclusion of all other thoughts and feelings. In many cases this will be enough to blot out the frightening paranormal perception. Repeat as often as necessary.

If the fixation on your higher power is not enough, visualise the frightening being cradled in a bubble of healing light between the very large hands of your higher power. Say to the being in your mind, 'I wish you to be happy and healed', and know that these good wishes will heal and erase all evil.

Here is a summary of how to deal with frightening paranormal perceptions:

Remedy for frightening paranormal experiences:

Know that paranormal experiences have arisen from your own unconscious mind and ignore them just like you would ignore a bad dream.

If you cannot ignore your frightening paranormal perceptions, fixate your mind on an image of your higher power. Focus so intensely that all other thoughts and perceptions are blotted out. Repeat as often as necessary.

Alternatively, visualise the frightening being within a bubble of loving light cradled between the hands of your higher power.

Remember that evil always comes from suffering and wish the evil being to be happy and healed with all your heart.

What follows are a few descriptions of typical frightening paranormal experiences and how to handle them:

Vivid dreams

During a kundalini awakening, nightmares can appear so vivid and intense that we may become convinced that they are real. But that is not the case because we have learnt from White Tara that nothing negative is real. A nightmare is always 'just a dream', no matter how intense and vivid it is. If we mistakenly assign reality to our nightmares, they may appear more and more real until they start dominating our life. Remember that in the world of the paranormal, our subjective feelings and the objective outer world become one.

On the other hand, if we experience positive and inspiring dreams we are encouraged to see them as real. We just need to be careful that the dream evokes more spiritual devotion and love in us rather than a sense of megalomania.

Sometimes people fear that their negative dreams are prophetic and will manifest. If you feel that way, my advice is to keep a diary of your dreams and check whether they come true or not. If they do not come true, you can relax in the knowledge that you do not have the prophetic gift.

> **Case study: Nigel, 33 years**
> Nigel was a client of mine who had experienced a very powerful kundalini awakening that had turned his world upside down. He repeatedly dreamt that an evil little man split his head open and inserted something dangerous into his brain. Nigel was totally convinced that these were real nightly visitations and experienced major panic.
>
> I explained to Nigel that a dream is 'just a dream', no matter how real and frightening it appears and that he should firmly reject all ideas that these vivid dreams were any more real than ordinary dreams.
>
> I also showed Nigel how to surround the evil little man with loving light and see him sitting between the hands of his higher power. Nigel's frightening dreams and fears were completely gone after a few weeks.

Horrific thoughts and visions

During waking hours some people experience horrific thoughts and visions, for example about torture or abuse. In these cases, I recommend fixing your mind on your higher power to the exclusion of all other thoughts until these ideas and images subside. You can also repeat a mantra or the name of your higher power in order to blot out these unwelcome thoughts. If we fully concentrate, there is only space for one thought in our mind and we should take advantage of this fact by using this method.

Unwelcome or painful clairvoyance

Some people are flooded with a form of clairvoyance that may feel unwelcome or painful - for example, reading other people's thoughts or becoming aware of their sexual feelings. We may also experience other people's pain as if it is our own, which can be confusing and painful. I myself frequently experience such perceptions but it took me years to fully understand them.

In order to distinguish clairvoyant experiences from our own, we need to become very observant. Here is the story of one of my own experiences that clarifies this point: When I was younger I became aware of the fact that I was always assaulted by intense depressive feelings whenever I entered the post office in the village where I lived at the time.

At first, I simply assumed that I was in a low mood myself but when I paid close attention I noticed that this dynamic also happened on days when I was really happy. I also noticed that it took roughly half an hour after leaving the post office before these feelings wore off.

I then started to look more carefully at the old couple that worked in the post office and tried to strike up some conversations with them in order to find out how they were feeling. The old man was a bit morose and not very friendly but he did not appear really depressed to me.

By comparison, the postman's wife, who sold gifts and stationery, appeared nice and friendly. It was only when I tried to sense with my heart towards her that I could sense a feeling of 'deadness' radiating out from her. After observing this dynamic carefully on several occasions, I could clearly tell that there was a very depressive atmosphere in the post office emanating mostly from the old lady which I 'caught' each time I walked in.

I then started to visualise the old couple in bubbles of love whenever I had to go to the post office. Doing this stopped the negative dynamic but I had to do my visualisation every time or else I would experience these negative feelings again. Eventually, the post office changed owners and the new postman was jolly and kind. It was a corroboration of my findings that I never had the depressive feelings again when I went into the post office.

As a general rule, observe yourself carefully before concluding that you are suffering from unwelcome clairvoyance. If you find that this is the case, see yourself and everybody else in bubbles of loving light.

Fear of the devil, psychic assault and possession

A number of my clients had feelings of being psychically assaulted by another person or by an invisible entity like the devil. If this is happening to you, you need to appreciate that another person or being can only ever have power over you if you are willing to give it to them. As I have explained before, on the level of psychic forces the boundaries between self and others blur and whatever we believe to be true will start to become real and manifest. Therefore, if you allow beliefs of being possessed or psychically assaulted to take hold of you, you are literally making yourself into a victim.

The first step towards letting go of these experiences is to firmly refuse to engage with them. Instead, you need to make it very clear to yourself that black magic and psychic assault can only ever have an effect on you if you allow this to happen.

In the next step, you can visualise yourself in a protective bubble of love and the being or person who you are afraid of in a separate bubble. You should then visualise this being in their bubble between the very big and loving hands of your higher power and wish this being to be healed and happy. You need to have this loving wish because their aggression can only have arisen from their own unhappiness and their connection to you can only have arisen from your own unhappiness. Therefore, if you want to be free of the connection to evil beings, you need to wish them to be happy from your deepest heart. This loving wish is the best psychic protection possible.

> **Case study; James, 44 years**
> James suffered very badly from the experience of psychic assault that he associated with an old friend he had known 20 years earlier. James was a devout Hindu from a branch of Hinduism that was very fatalistic and demanded that everybody should simply put up with everything 'as God's will', even if it brought great suffering.
> I showed James how to visualise his old friend in a bubble of love resting in the hands of his favourite God Ganesha.
> At first, James made good progress but then he stopped his practice. When I asked him why he had stopped he explained that he could not accept this practice, as he believed it to be against the fatalistic religious teaching of complete surrender. Sadly, there was not much I could do for James and he continued to suffer.
> Other clients in a similar situation were able to completely let of these experiences of psychic assault by sending love.

Channelling disorder

People who are interested in channelling and mediumship are at greater risk of developing a channelling disorder once their kundalini is awakened. This is simply due to the fact that kundalini amplifies all our inner experiences. What felt like a manageable experience may appear as a kind of possession after the kundalini has been awakened.

The general advice for channelling problems is to stop all these activities. Instead, focus on your higher power alone because it is the highest source of love and wisdom in the universe and the only safe being to channel. By comparison, opening your psychic doors to spirit guides, angels and deceased relatives may inadvertently draw in lower energies, which can make you very scared. Note that these energies can only come in if we give them permission and that they cannot do this from their own side alone.

The danger of commercialising a supernatural power
When someone has developed a fantastic supernatural power like spiritual healing, clairvoyance or the ability to fascinate others with their spiritual presence, they can easily be tempted to try making money with their gift. However, there are certain dangers attached to this. White Tara explains:

> *It is dangerous to try making money with a supernatural power because the line of truth and cheating can be very thin. Powers like spiritual healing or clairvoyant reading will only work if you are in a good state of mind but once you are making money with it, you will be tempted to exercise them no matter what state of mind you are in. That is of course cheating and will bring bad karma.*

I had clients who got themselves into trouble by trying to make money from their supernatural gifts. The problem was that they could not continue their work due to their debilitating kundalini symptoms and they were desperate for me to help them get back to their money-earning powers.

Here is what I do myself to address this problem: I have become quite clairvoyant due to my kundalini process and had ample opportunity to test the accuracy of my perceptions in the work with my clients. I like to use my clairvoyance in the work with my clients because it helps me to come to the root of what is troubling them more quickly. However, when my clients specifically ask me for a clairvoyant reading and particularly for a fortune telling, I refuse. I explain to them that I only charge them for the psychotherapeutic treatment and that all my clairvoyant readings are for free. In that way, I only do clairvoyant readings when I want to do them and I am never under pressure to perform when I do not feel up to it.

So, if you are a massage therapist or healer of some sort, you can work in the same way. Charge for the 'ordinary aspect' of your work and give your supernatural ability for free and at your own discretion.

Breakdown experiences
Now we come to the aspect of kundalini that most people will find most frightening – the so-called breakdown experiences. However, I would like to reassure you right from the start that nothing really breaks down during these experiences other than our false and illusory ideas about ourselves. Even though these experiences may be rather uncomfortable, they are not dangerous and certainly not signs of mental

disease. We will come to the so-called kundalini psychosis in a minute and I will show you that it has not much in common with ordinary mental disease.

Dark night of the soul

In the spiritual literature there are references to the so-called 'dark night of the soul'. St John of the Cross coined this term and Evelyn Underhill explored it in depth in her book 'Mysticism'. In short, it means a prolonged experience of running out of any luck and experiencing problems in every area of life.

These 'bad stretches' can happen to anyone, even without kundalini, but with active kundalini they can happen in a rather pronounced and perplexing way. I certainly wondered whether I was having a 'dark night' when my career came to a total standstill and I felt more and more alienated from the world for almost seven years. But as you remember from my story at the beginning of chapter five, I was not particularly unhappy during this time and experienced states of intense ecstasy and bliss virtually every day. When I asked White Tara about this she told me:

> *Kundalini accelerates your development and in that way also hastens the ripening of your karma. Therefore, the more kundalini you have, the more challenges you need to overcome, which is a good thing if you want to reach enlightenment fast.*

White Tara also gave me this advice about how to deal with this situation:

> *Through the dark night you are taught that bliss alone is not enough and that you also need the loving union with the deity. Once you can fully unite in love with a deity and let go of any resentment about the rejection of others, the dark night will be over.*

> *In order to end the dark night you need to send love to the very people who are rejecting you. Therefore, love and the heart chakra are most important to overcome the dark night.*

So yet again, White Tara tells us that we need to focus more on love. This can be challenging during the dark night because we may find ourselves very alone during this time and feel as if other people and maybe even our higher power have forsaken us. Yet the challenge is to keep our heart open and send love to everyone who has hurt us and to the world in general.

So-called kundalini 'psychosis'

I am in agreement with other experts of kundalini like Lee Sannella and Yvonne Kason that the so-called 'kundalini-psychosis' is a misnomer because it has, in fact, little in common with the textbook mental disease called psychosis. However, if someone has several of the symptoms that I have described in this chapter, it can result in a crisis that may look to the untrained eye like a complete breakdown or psychosis.

The person may be flooded with paranormal visions and voices, they may have the sensations of snakes gyrating in their lower abdomen, they may feel extremely frightened and to top it all off they may suffer from insomnia, which can bring on mild hallucinations. All this may look like mental disease but there are certain factors that distinguish a kundalini crisis from true mental disease and psychosis:

People in a kundalini crisis usually maintain a functioning sense of self that realises that something is wrong and will seek help. People with ordinary psychosis do not notice that something is wrong because their entire mind is taken up by psychotic thoughts. They do not seek help and they also often resist help.

A person with a kundalini crisis can usually pinpoint the exact time and trigger of the beginning of their crisis. In most cases the trigger was intensive spiritual practice. By contrast, ordinary psychosis usually develops slowly and gradually and the patient cannot remember a healthy sense of self.

A person in a kundalini crisis can remember what it is like to feel 'normal' and wishes to go back to this state, while a psychotic patient has lost touch with their healthy state of mind.

People in a kundalini crisis can talk about what is going on their mind and usually they also *want* to talk about this. People with ordinary psychosis rarely want to talk about the content of their psychotic mind.

People in a kundalini crisis usually feel a strong urge to make their life more loving, healthy and spiritual. In people with ordinary psychosis this is usually not the case and often these patients turn away from a healthy life-style, loving relationships and spirituality.

In my experience, psychosis-like breakdowns do not happen very often in people with active kundalini. They are most likely to happen when someone has a history of drug taking. In my own clinical experience, I have observed that frequent drug use – even if it was years in the past – seems to make a severe kundalini crisis more likely. I have also observed that ex-drug users sometimes 'swap' the drugs for the intense highs and low of a kundalini awakening and become attached to all this turmoil. Sometimes, they also use indiscriminate visits to energy healers to get more 'experiences' in a similar way to taking drugs, which can have disastrous consequences for their over-sensitive mind.

On the Internet you can find the most horrendous stories of people suffering from kundalini-psychosis but in my therapy practice I have never witnessed truly hopeless situations. Usually, people get better fairly quickly by stopping the things that aggravate them (e.g. going to energy healers or doing breathing exercises) and working with higher-consciousness healing.

> **Case-study: Gary, 34 years**
> Gary is a highly intelligent accountant who came to see me because he had some sort of breakdown caused by kundalini. Gary had a history of heavy drug taking but had given up the drugs after a very painful break-up with his girlfriend two years earlier.
>
> He then went travelling to Bali where he became acquainted with spiritual ideas and the concept of kundalini. He visited many healers and spiritual teachers but did not engage in a sound spiritual practice. Instead, he 'consumed' different forms of healings in a haphazard way, much like he used to take drugs without ever considering the risks of doing so.
>
> Once Gary arrived back home he started to develop strange fears and kundalini-like symptoms, which he tried to counteract through cathartic outbursts. He also continued going to many different energy healers. Gary spent hours and hours 'letting his feelings out' but his symptoms grew steadily worse until he was engulfed with frightening visions and unable to go to work.
>
> I explained to Gary that the forceful expression of emotions was greatly exacerbating his symptoms and that it would be wise to stop this form of self-made therapy. I also strongly advised him to stop seeing energy healers as both these avenues of self-healing were actually making him worse. Gary only very reluctantly agreed because he was virtually addicted to doing these things.
>
> We then worked through the many guilt-feelings that surfaced for Gary as he had hurt numerous people throughout the years of his drug taking. Doing this was not easy for Gary who had always chosen the 'easy route' of numbing his

feelings through his various approaches of thrill seeking.

During the months that Gary worked with me, he steadily grew more stable and we ended the sessions once he was ready to go back to work.

Chapter seven
The Deity-State

Now we are coming to the very essence what the kundalini process is all about – the deity-state. The deity-state is a synonym for enlightenment but the phrase deity-state makes it clearer that we are aiming for the union with the divine and not for some sort of self-made enlightenment. Tibetan Buddhism teaches that full enlightenment cannot be reached simply through practicing the right technique but can only be achieved through our complete surrender to the deity. In Western terminology we are speaking of an act of grace.

What is the deity-state?
Generally speaking, in the deity-state our old identity is completely gone and has been replaced with a very clear and real sense of actually being the deity. This is not some sort of imagination but an actual experience. The Dalai Lama says: "In short, the body of the Buddha is achieved through meditating on it."

I have asked White Tara many questions about the deity-state and I carefully compared her answers to the teachings I received from my Buddhist teachers over the past 30 years. This is what she has to teach us and, to the best of my knowledge, it is fully compatible with Tibetan Buddhist teachings. She says:

> *Uniting with the deity is the pinnacle of the spiritual path. It is what all human beings have to achieve in order to come to the higher worlds.*

The 'almost-union' of bliss and love
White Tara teaches that the deity-state is the 'almost-union' between the sea of love and the bliss of kundalini. She explains:

> *Enlightenment is not a non-dual experience or Samadhi. Non-duality implies non-movement – a state of complete frozenness. Instead, there is a subtle back and forth between the sea of love, which is felt more in the upper chakras, and the bliss of kundalini that is felt more in the lower chakras - without ever getting stuck in one of these poles as the ego does.*

In the ego-state you see love and happiness as incompatible. Love is seen as self-sacrifice and happiness is seen as selfishness. Even in the deity-state these two aspects never completely merge - they just become more and more united in an ever-increasing harmony.

The most important point in these teachings is that enlightenment or the deity-state is a dynamic experience. We alternate between love and bliss, which are situated in the upper and lower chakras in one harmonic movement. Doing this will create a beautiful vibration just as a vibration of a string in a musical instrument produces a beautiful sound. It is this vibration that is the deity-state and not a state of oneness without movement or dynamic.

White Tara explains that in our ordinary ego-state we have a tendency to get stuck either in the pole of being loving and self-sacrificing to the detriment of being happy and successful, or we over-focus on our own pleasure and success to the detriment of caring for others. It is only when we bring love and happiness into one harmonic state that we find final satisfaction. Doing this is a continuous *process* - without getting fixated on one position.

You may remember that we have already discussed in chapter four the fact that most people have a tendency to reside either more in their higher chakras (love and ideals) or in the lower chakras (happiness, sex, success and power). Enlightenment means a cessation of being stuck in one pole and instead involves balancing the love in the higher chakras and the joy in the lower chakras in the most harmonic way.

For me, it was also very interesting to learn that love and happiness in the upper and lower chakras can never be completely united but that the highest state is a harmonious alternation between those two aspects of our being.

In Tibetan Buddhism this two-fold aspect of enlightenment is expressed in the teaching that enlightenment is like a bird with two wings – one wing is for compassion (love) and the other wing is for wisdom (joy, happiness, success, power). Only if both wings are fully developed can our bird take off and fly.

The experience of love in the deity-state

White Tara explained to me in great detail the experience of love in the deity-state. She said:

The deity expresses her love in three different ways: Firstly, there is simple

> and sheer benevolence without a specific intention that envelops everybody in love without ever rejecting anybody. This is her basic and on-going attitude for all phenomena and beings. In other words, the deity experiences everybody and everything in her own heart.
>
> The second expression of love is the intention to heal. The deity does not always send healing love to everyone because this would mean imposing herself onto others. The deity gives this kind of love to people when they ask for it and when the karmic conditions are right.
>
> The third expression of love is ecstatic union. This happens spontaneously when the deity encounters people whose love and devotion are pure. As a result of the uniting experience, a huge amount of energy is set free as in a nuclear fusion and both beings arise as the Buddha.

For our own wish to become enlightened, the third aspect is the most exciting. It says that once our own love and devotion is pure, the deity will unite with us and as a result we will arise as a Buddha. We can see here quite clearly the combination of having to work on our chakras on the one hand and having devotion to the deity on the other hand in order to reach enlightenment.

The life force of the deity

White Tara teaches about the life force of the deity:

> The deity has an unlimited capacity to love but she does not have an unlimited amount of life energy. Even Buddhas need to preserve and replenish their energy. Deities have more energy than humans but it is still a reservoir that can become depleted and needs to be replenished.
>
> This is why the deity cannot awaken others against their will by dominating their energy field with love, as this would cost too much energy. If it were possible, they would have long ago done so.
>
> The deity replenishes her energy – just like everybody else – through loving union with others who appreciate this union. So, when you unite with the deity, you both replenish your energies through this loving encounter.

The last few paragraphs from White Tara explain why divine beings do not interfere more in human affairs and why they do not prevent all the suffering that is so prevalent here on earth. In order to receive help and healing from a deity, we ourselves have to do everything we can to purify ourselves from our selfish impulses and humbly ask for help. Only then can we receive the full blessing of the deity.

Sense of self in the deity-state

White Tara explained to me about the sense of self of the deity:

> In the deity-state you experience everything within your own heart because it expands infinitely. Other beings are simultaneously others but they are also part of you. In practice, this means you 'are' a universe of love and you invite all other beings in.
>
> Even when the deity unites with others in love, she is simultaneously aware of her separate identity. Therefore, there is no fear of being annihilated by this experience, as people would feel in the ego-state.
>
> In the ego-state your happiness gets threatened by the suffering of others, but once your love and bliss is strong enough, you can experience the suffering of other beings and your bliss simultaneously.
>
> As a deity you still have some sort of personal character because the deity-state is the result of a long succession of wishes, which colour your identity. Everybody's journey towards enlightenment is different because people have certain favourite topics that they explore in more depth until they reach enlightenment. Some people focus more on intellectual inquiry while others focus on art, wisdom or service. These different interests result in different characters in enlightened beings.
>
> In the deity-state you assume a pure body made from light that is invisible to most others. Along the middle of the deity-body there is the central channel radiating with light like a white egg. This is the essence of the deity-state. It is like a power station that you can use to create reality. This is the light body.

> *The light body is made of white golden light that peters out at the boundaries and is as big as your outstretched hands. This light body can be projected anywhere it is needed and you may do with it whatever you want – healing or teaching. In that way your effect on people will magnify.*
>
> *If you can combine the deity experience with the heat of the kundalini in the abdomen, you manifest as the deity 'in the flesh' and only then can you also be recognised by others as the deity. We call this the 'manifested deity'. Without kundalini, the deity-state remains an internal meditation experience.*

I found it very interesting to learn that others can only recognise enlightenment in someone else if that someone has sufficient kundalini. Without the kundalini we may have the enlightenment experience within ourselves but others will continue to see us as ordinary people.

Intention at the deity-state

When discussing intention at the deity-state we need to remember that the life force or kundalini is essentially desire. So, noone is ever without desire or intention, whether unenlightened or enlightened. What changes are the objects of our desire and the concentration of the life force that we can use to manifest our desires. While the ego desires things and people solely for its own self-aggrandisement and uses its desire energy in a haphazard and chaotic way, the deity's desires are purely based on love and are used like a highly concentrated laser beam. This is what White Tara has to say:

> *Even though you are complete and whole in the deity-state, this state is neither passive nor devoid of desire. You continue to desire to help other beings and to unite with them lovingly because this is the nature of your divine essence. The ego wants to unite out of a sense of deficiency while the deity wants to unite out of a surplus of love and the desire to heal.*
>
> *In the deity-state all your desires are directed on to love, which means you have purely loving wishes. In other words, the sea of love and the desire, or kundalini, is perfectly balanced.*

The desire of the deity feels very different to the desire of the ego because it is completely and eternally fulfilled. In that sense, we can say that in the deity-state you do not have goals. Your love and desire have merged and give you eternal satisfaction.

I found White Tara's teaching about deities having desires confusing at first because, after all, the Buddha said in his second noble truth that all suffering is due to desire. However, we need to remember that the life force itself is essentially desire. We also need to distinguish between the ego's desires, which all lead to suffering, and the desires of the deity, which are based on love and lead to happiness.

When the Buddha said in his second noble truth that all our suffering is caused by desire he meant the many addictions and unhealthy desires we have. By contrast, the tantric path to enlightenment through kundalini means that we use pure desire energy (kundalini) to merge with the sea of love and thus reach enlightenment.

Perception of the world in the deity-state

In Tibetan Buddhism there is the teaching of the 'pure view' that says that Buddhas 'hear all sounds as mantras' and 'see all beings as Buddhas'. I always found this teaching very intriguing and even more so when I was in the phase of my auditory oversensitivity. In my experience then, my perception of the world was getting worse rather than better, which made we wonder if had 'lost the plot' spiritually speaking. However, I am relieved to report that, as time went on, this trend stopped and nowadays I have frequent experiences of seeing breath-taking beauty around me. White Tara explains:

Through the continuous experience of blissful love every sense contact of the deity becomes an experience of ecstasy. You - including all of your perceptions - are all-pervading blissful love. This process is accompanied by a perception of extreme beauty. This experience cannot be manufactured but happens of its own accord just like the deity-state itself. It is called the 'pure view' or 'seeing the world as a paradise'.

Despite seeing the world as a paradise, the deity is still aware of beings who suffer and misbehave. But she understands that all this happens out of ignorance and wishes the very best for everybody. She sees all beings as her dearly beloved children.

In the deity-state you are never alone. You are always surrounded by your divine mandala full of loving beings who desire your blessings and ecstatic union. If you have enough kundalini, this mandala will manifest in the 'real world'; otherwise it will stay at the mind level.

Once again, White Tara points out that without enough kundalini we can only experience this wonderful view during our meditation. Unfortunately, this increases the risk of rebound depression and anger that we have already discussed in chapter six. White Tara explains it like this:

If you can experience bliss and love only in the top chakras, you can get an idea of the 'world as paradise' only in meditation. But after meditation your pure view can be violently disturbed by other people because you still lack the power of your lower chakras. Only through the navel chakra are you able to influence your environment in a way that makes the 'pure view' more than a meditation experience.

'Practising' the deity-state

Strictly speaking, the deity-state is not a meditation and it cannot be practised. However, for the lack of an appropriate word I will continue to speak of 'practising' but will put the word into quotation marks to emphasise that this is not some technique. White Tara told me:

The deity-state cannot be achieved through a technique. It arises spontaneously out of our bliss, kundalini and devotion. However, there are certain steps that can be practised to make this spontaneous transformation more likely.

I will now outline the steps that are necessary to facilitate the spontaneous event of merging with the deity. You can think about this process as being like falling in love - no matter how much we want it, there is nothing we can do to force or 'achieve' falling in love. However, there are certain conditions, such as having good self-confidence and a kind caring attitude, which will make this wonderful event more likely.

Deepen the experience of non-self

The most important prerequisite to 'achieving' the deity-state is the deepening of our blissful spacious experience of non-self. We have already touched upon this topic in chapters three and four. White Tara says:

> *If bliss is practised correctly, it is an inner experience of loving blissful space. This means uniting in love with your divine essence in its virgin state – before anything has arisen from it.*

The loving blissful space that we experience when we open our chakras is an experience of non-self. When we are in this state, we can notice that everything we took to be our identity – our history, characteristics and achievements – becomes more and more unimportant and somehow 'flimsy'. Whether we had a happy or unhappy past, whether we are thin or fat or whether we are a high-achiever or an under-achiever, we will get a sense that we are really not defined by any of these things, which appeared so solid before.

In fact, we notice that we can define ourselves any way we like. Just like an actor can take on different identities, we can suddenly see that we have the choice to take on the identity of a high-achiever, if we were under-achieving before, or vice versa. The traumas of our past that felt so limiting before suddenly become distant memories, which do not evoke any real emotions anymore. And we also notice that we can change all our negative characteristics into positive ones simply by deciding to do so. We can do this because we realise that we are not set in stone, that we have the freedom to change anyway we like because, ultimately, we are simply space.

Feeling that on the deepest level we are simply space enables us to truly merge with and identify with the deity. By contrast, if we still believe we have a personal self that is defined by outer conditions or by our past, it will be impossible to take on the identity of the deity. That would be like saying to an ice-cube 'try to be like water' when the ice-cube still believes in its icy and hard character. It can never work. But once the ice-cube realises that its innermost nature is luminous space it can let go from the tensions that have compressed it into an ice-cube and relax into being water. In the same way, as long as we believe ourselves to be a 'person with certain characteristics', we can never allow the deity to 'take us over'. We would be unable to accept this because we would be too afraid of being annihilated in the process or we would feel too undeserving to allow it.

Once we go more deeply into the spacious quality of our blissful mind, we can literally relax the tensions and fears that have moulded us into the limited person that we have been up to now and recognise ourselves for what we truly are - blissful space without core and with boundaries that expand into infinity. Once we have thoroughly familiarised ourselves with this experience of non-self, we can take on the identity of the deity.

Arising as the deity

At some point, while resting in the bliss of non-self, something wonderful will happen. You will suddenly experience yourself as a fully-formed deity – glorious, beautiful, bedecked with the most precious ornaments and exuding nothing but the most blissful love.

This experience cannot be manufactured but happens spontaneously, just like the bliss arose spontaneously in the first place when you deeply relaxed your chakras. In the beginning, these moments of being the deity may last no longer than a second but, as time goes on, you will be able to experience the deity-state for longer and longer periods of time

There are certain techniques we can use to make this moment of arising as the deity more likely. In Tibetan Buddhism it is said that guru-yoga or deity-yoga – the union with an enlightened teacher or deity – is the fastest and easiest way to become enlightened. In fact, people who have a great deal of devotion do not need any other practice or complicated spiritual teachings apart from this most powerful approach.

Uniting with the deity has been known in many different religious traditions and is the essence of what is supposed to happen at the Christian ritual of communion. And indeed, merging with Christ was the main practice of medieval saints like Catherine of Siena and Theresa of Avila, which catapulted these women onto the highest spiritual states and enabled them to develop many supernatural powers in a relatively short time. Here are White Tara's teachings:

> *Uniting with the deity in love is the fastest way to achieve and stabilise the deity-state. You can never 'enlighten' yourself because your limiting ego-ideas would never allow that. If you were to try to 'talk yourself' into an enlightened confidence, it would result in megalomania.*

So White Tara is making an important distinction between the deity-state that happens spontaneously or by grace, and the use of a 'technique' of forcefully visualising ourselves as the deity. What we are aiming at here is of course the first option. We should always try to let things unfold naturally and avoid the second option of manufacturing the process in some way.

White Tara also explains that it is even more powerful to unite with a deity who has incarnated as a human being than with a deity who has never incarnated. She says:

> *You can unite with a celestial being but uniting with an enlightened human master is more powerful for stabilising the deity-state. It will change you more quickly. When you unite with an enlightened master, their love and your love unites and that is the fastest way to reach enlightenment.*

How can we 'achieve' this wonderful union with the deity? White Tara gives us this simple advice that I have 'practiced' with wonderful results myself:

> *When you want to unite with the deity or the enlightened teacher you simply open yourself up and gently call the deity towards you while being completely open and undefended.*

> *You focus on one chakra after the other while maintaining the union with the deity or enlightened teacher. You start with the crown chakra and call on the deity. The deity will then descend into you from there - chakra by chakra.*

What uniting with the deity feels like

Everyone who has had higher spiritual states will tell you that it is very difficult to describe these experiences in ordinary language. But I will nevertheless try to do so and please forgive me if my words are woefully inadequate:

First you feel like blissful, open space. Your old sense of identity disappears and you feel as free and joyful as a bird flying in playful abandon through a space of radiant, glittering, joyful light.

Then suddenly and seemingly out of nowhere, you 'arise' as a fully-formed deity in an instant. With your inner eye you can see that you are utterly beautiful and adorned with the most precious jewels and ornaments. Your mind is in a state of the most exalted bliss. It does not produce any thoughts but is in a state of pure love that you give to the beings that surround you in your divine mandala. You have so much love for these beings that you feel they are literally residing in your heart that is as big as the universe.

You feel blissful energy meandering through your being like rivers of the sweetest and most delicious nectar. These rivers of bliss may go up and down your spine, into your arms and legs and through all the chakras. Wherever this energy goes, it unfolds like the most beautiful flowers and produces visions of love, peace and serenity as if you yourself are a paradise.

You are always surrounded by a myriad of beings with whom you unite in deepest love. Your inner bliss and your outer surrounding merge into one blissful and loving experience that can be so extreme that tears of rapture run down your face and your body contorts into ecstatic postures.

The question may arise of whether the experience of being the deity is just a figment of imagination or if it is real. Lama Yeshe answers this question in his book 'Introduction to Tantra' on pages 122 and 123. He says: *"When you see yourself as a deity, you should feel that you are the real emanation of the deity. Don't think that you are just pretending; you should be convinced. Then, like the actor who remains in character even after the play is finished, you might surprise yourself to find that you have actually become the deity. Such divine pride – the strong sense of actually being the deity – is crucial. With it, tantric transformation will come naturally and be very powerful. Those people who think that tantric transformation is only involved with pretending to be a deity are completely mistaken."*

As I have explained before, the 'deity-practice' is not really a practice but is more like the process of falling in love, which cannot be forced. Nevertheless, you can gently experiment with visualising yourself as the deity because doing this will make the real experience more likely to occur.

Using kundalini to achieve the manifested deity-state

As we have discussed before, kundalini is an amplifier of what is going on in our mind – good and bad. So, if we combine the 'deity-practice' with kundalini, the effect will be more powerful and tangible. White Tara explains:

> *Kundalini practice and the deity practice reinforce each other and ideally should always be practiced together.*
>
> *Without kundalini your deity-practice cannot stabilise. You may experience the deity-state for short moments in the meditation but if you want to*

stabilise it and also be recognised as the deity by others, you need to combine it with kundalini.

Kundalini makes our meditation experiences more stable so that we can experience the deity-state for longer and more intensely. Kundalini will also enable us to be recognised as the deity by others, which is important if we want to teach others. How does all this look this in practice? White Tara tells us:

In the beginning you may have to go deliberately from the kundalini in your lower body to the deity experience in your upper body and back again. But with training you will eventually be able to hold these states in your mind more and more simultaneously. Eventually, you can simply use a mantra or a symbol to evoke the manifested deity-state instantaneously.

It is important to understand that when White Tara says 'in the beginning' this means many years for most of us. So, we have to settle into a practice of going up and down in our body-mind and alternate between the blissful deity-state that manifests mostly in the head, throat and heart and the blissful kundalini heat that manifests in the lower abdomen.

We can visualise going up and down our spine or within our central channel or we can imagine an oval circle where the energy rises in the spine and comes down again in the front of the body. But we should avoid going up and down in the front the body as this can throw up problems as we have discussed before. By now, you obviously know that nothing really rises or comes down – these are just visualisations which will help us to unite our most profound discrepancy between the love of the upper chakras and the power passions of the lower chakras.

Once again, it is important to remember that this up and down between the higher and lower chakras should not be done in a mechanical way but with much feeling and awareness. For example, we may rest for a minute or two in the abdomen until we feel a natural rising up of the energy, then we follow the energy up to the brain and rest in the blissful experience of the deity-state with our surrounding mandala for however long we can maintain our concentration. Once we feel an impulse we let the energy descend to the navel again and repeat the whole circle. There are no hard and fast rules about how long we should stay in each of the two poles but we should spend roughly an equal amount of time in the upper chakras and in the lower chakras.

Being quite impatient myself, I thought it would be most beneficial to stay in the union with the deity as long as possible but White Tara does not agree.

> *You do not unite with the deity and then cling. 'Only union' or 'only separation' are just two different forms of pain. When you are united with the deity, soon there is a stirring that asks for separation. And once you are separated you want to unite again. So there is a natural rhythm between bliss and deity-state that you can completely trust. It is this back and forth that is the right way – not the endless attempt of staying in one pole. It is a mistake to only want to unite.*
>
> *Over time, the 'gap' between your old ego-identity and the deity-state will become smaller and eventually it will completely disappear – like drops of milk falling into water will make the water more and more like milk.*

The complete 'deity-practice'

Preparation

Resolve to do the 'deity-practice' for the best of all beings.

Visualise your body as hollow and filled with brilliant light and generate bliss in all the chakras one by one, including the navel chakra, as you have learnt in chapters four and five.

Gently allow the kundalini to rise up from your navel as you have learnt in chapter five.

Continue to let the kundalini rise until the bliss is strong and beautiful in all the chakras and you experience the spacious and blissful state of non-self.

Arising as the deity

While resting in the bliss of non-self you will spontaneously experience short moments of actually being the deity. You will feel this experience mostly in the upper body.

Alternatively, imagine your deity in front of you filled with and surrounded by beautiful light. The deity is smiling at you with deepest love and you feel that he or she wishes you to be happy and enlightened. Feel devotion, gratefulness and love.

Gently call your deity towards yourself by their name and open yourself like you would open yourself towards a person you have totally fallen in love with. Imagine your chakras opening wide to receive the deity.

Feel the light-body of the deity entering into your light-body and feel that this merging transforms you into the deity. Feel that you are as beautiful, blissful and loving as the deity.

See yourself surrounded by your divine mandala filled with beings you love like your dearly beloved children. Your love is so strong that you feel that all these people are literally residing in your heart that is as wide as the universe.

Uniting the kundalini with the deity-state

Tune into the joyful heat in your abdomen as you have learnt in chapter five and let the energy rise. As the energy rises to your higher chakras, tune into the deity-state and see yourself surrounded by your divine mandala.

Stay in the deity-state and allow it to unfold in beautiful visions and energy sensations until your mind starts to wander.

Then focus on your lower body again until the kundalini rises and once again tune into the deity-state. Roughly spend an equal amount of time in both sets of chakras.

Remember to focus simultaneously on your surrounding divine mandala filled with beings you love dearly while doing this meditation.

Respond to all your thoughts as the deity. If you think about a certain person, see this person enveloped in divine love. If you think about a project, see this project develop in the most wonderful way for the best of all beings. If you feel pain in your body, see and feel pulsating divine light in this part of your body. If you want to help and heal a certain person, see their body filled and surrounded with pulsating divine light. Whatever thought arises in your mind, make it part of your 'deity-practice'.

Ending the meditation

End your meditation practice by dedicating all its merit for the benefit of all beings.

Challenges to 'achieving' the deity-state

'Deity-practice' is the pinnacle of all spiritual approaches and I wish I could tell you that there are no more challenges once you have reached this stage. But there is one drawback that I feel obliged to share with you. White Tara told me:

> *There will be a severe time of testing before the deity unites with you. She*

will only do so if you are completely purified and for that reason 'sends' you some tests. These tests basically consist of withholding the fulfilment of your wishes. In that way, all your negativities that you have not dealt with will come to the surface.

If you can go through this 'empty phase' and maintain your unconditional bliss, then the deity will deem you worthy of the union with her. Once you can unite with the deity you know that the testing phase is over and that the enlightenment phase has started.

'Practicing' the deity-state in daily life
Here is White Tara's advice about 'practising' the deity-state in daily life:

In the beginning you focus on the deity-state only in the meditation and during daily life you focus simply on the bliss. There is a danger that you will become megalomaniac if you focus on the deity-state in daily life too early. But with time you can also practice the deity-state during daily life.

So, we should continue to go back and forth between the bliss of the lower and upper chakras as we have learnt in the previous section but we should not forcefully visualise ourselves as the deity. The obvious question is, of course, how would we know when the danger of becoming megalomaniac has subsided and when we are ready to 'practice' the union with the deity in daily life? The answer is that you need to let it come naturally. 'Practice' uniting with your deity in your meditation and if you find that this practice spontaneously spills over into the time after your meditation, then the time is right.

However, you should carefully test yourself to determine whether 'being the deity' in daily life makes you more loving and compassionate or less. Visualising ourselves prematurely or forcefully as the deity can derail into a gigantic ego-trip. Make sure you ask your family and friends whether you have become more loving or whether you have become more arrogant and harsh. Take this feedback seriously! If you are told that you appear more prideful and angry, immediately back off and practice more loving-kindness. If you have moved on to higher practices too early before you have thoroughly dismantled your ego, there is always the opportunity of going back and filling in your missing gaps. White Tara elucidates further:

> *The change resulting from achieving the deity-state is gradual and will accumulate over time. That is why you may not feel it as a distinct step. The bliss of kundalini is like a distinct rung on a ladder. The deity-practice is more like stepping off the ladder into a new realm.*

If you can experience the deity-state in meditation but it does not seem to spill over into your daily life, then you have too little kundalini. White Tara told me:

> *It can be disconcerting to discover that you can enter into the deity-state quite easily during meditation but revert to much lower states of consciousness outside the meditation. In order to overcome this problem, you need more kundalini.*

Everything that we have discussed about rebound anger and depression after blissful states in chapter six also applies to the deity meditation experiences. If you do not have enough kundalini and your ordinary life is still in stark contrast to your blissful meditation, you will have to focus more on the navel in order to close this gap.

Uniting your desires with the deity

The question may arise about how we can unite our human desires with the desires of the deity. White Tara explains:

> *When you first unite with the deity, she may feel very passive because she rests more in the sea of love and that may make you feel disconnected from 'your' desires. As a result, your desires may even more forcefully re-assert themselves.*

In order to integrate our desires with the desires of the deity, White Tara advises:

> *You simply combine your desires with the deity-state. If your desires are not in alignment with the deity, they will extinguish this state. If your desires are in harmony with the deity-state, they will enhance and enliven this state and they will also come true much more quickly.*
>
> *In other words, you are never completely taken over by the deity. You just*

merge more and more but you can always bring in your own desires – in perfect harmony.

Maintaining the deity-state makes you more serene and spiritually content. All your spiritual questions will be answered and there is nothing more to discover on a personal level. You have left 'yourself' with all your problems behind.

If you can unite with the deity, all your siddhis and powers will gradually grow and you can have everything you want that is in harmony with the deity-state. However, you need to be patient because these changes will be gradual.

The manifested deity-state

White Tara calls the final stabilisation of the deity the 'manifested deity-state'. She explains:

The kundalini energy first rises to the head and then descends into the heart. When the energy goes to the heart, the deity manifests for others to see.

One outcome of the manifested deity-state is the light-body. You experience your body filled with blissful light that radiates to all sides as bright and as powerful as a sun. You can use this light-body to perform many supernatural feats and develop all your siddhis.

The final stabilisation of the deity-state will happen on its own accord at an unpredictable time. It will happen in a gradual way and not all at once. The difference between what you feel is your 'usual self' and the experience of uniting with the deity in the meditation will gradually become less and less. At some point, the two states will become one and the deity-state will become more and more solid and finally completely stable.

The full stabilisation of the deity-state is not likely to happen in the human world but only in the higher worlds. You can then return to the human world with the enlightenment stage fully formed. This has only happened to a handful of people who have incarnated in human history. These beings have voluntarily lowered their vibrations out of compassion so that they are very similar to the human state.

So, White Tara encourages us to keep raising our kundalini and merging with the deity but she also tells us that the final stabilisation of the union with the deity is not likely to happen within this lifetime. In that sense, we are all pilgrims who are walking together towards our final destination of becoming fully divine.

I am grateful that you have been walking with me up to this point and would enjoy hearing what you made of this book. You could write a review of this book on your blog or on one of the Amazon sites. Or you could contact me via my website at www.taraspringett.com to let me know your thoughts about this book.

Final note:

If you need any further help and guidance, please do not hesitate to contact me via my website www.taraspringett.com or email me at tara@taraspringett.com.

Appendix
Testimonials for Kundalini Healing

These are testimonials from clients who came to see me because they suffered from kundalini symptoms. I have changed people's names to ensure anonymity.

Michael, 31 years
During the autumn of 2013 I had a very strong kundalini experience, which completely derailed my life. During a longer period of time I had paralysing fears and insomnia. Tara has helped me a lot to understand the nature of the kundalini and she also gave me methods to overcome the insomnia and anxiety. A big part of the anxiety in my kundalini process was due to the ignorance of how the kundalini affects my mind. Through Tara's explanations I was able to understand the kundalini as a part of myself and integrate it. In that way, I could overcome my fears.

Andrew, 31 years
I contacted Tara because I was experiencing an uncomfortable feeling in my body during my meditation and mindfulness exercises. Sometimes I could feel a strong energy going up and down my body giving me a feeling of anxiety and panic and even pain at times. Tara helped me to see what was going on, she offered kind, clear and gentle insights and explained to me a new way to understand the energy and my feelings. She has been particularly helpful using tools and visualization techniques to teach me how to progress in my psychological and spiritual growth. It's a fact that within few months Tara gave me some powerful strategies, which enabled me to cope with many situations and understand myself better.

Alison, 33 years
I am feeling well. I have found our sessions very, very helpful! The breath work for anxiety was particularly helpful. I am continuing to practice your manifesting and breathing techniques and they are really effective.

Juliet, 58 years
The journey of kundalini energy can be very lonely and at times frightening. Finding Tara was like finding a ray of light at the end of the tunnel. Not only is she compassionate and kind but turns what seems like madness into sanity and has a very down to earth approach to the whole process using her own unique healing method. I could not recommend her more highly.

Arthur, 49 years
In the fall of 1997 I was blessed with a profound Kundalini awakening that has dramatically transformed my life. I am deeply grateful to have found Tara; her experiential knowledge of Kundalini has been extremely helpful.

Through Tara's guidance, specifically the practice of her unique higher consciousness healing method, I have come to a much greater understanding of the blessings of Kundalini as well as how to develop a healthy relationship with this gift. What is of most benefit to me is Tara's gentle teachings that point to love as the foundation of all healing. Thank you Tara for your wisdom.

John, 35 years
I don't believe in miracles but the 'Five minute miracle' works. After going through a powerful and disorientating kundalini awakening finding Tara was the anchor back to reality and the beginning of a clearer understanding of what was happening. Her healing techniques and advice got me grounded and strong again. I whole-heartedly recommend Tara Springett.

Jane, 41 years
I am doing well and using your exercise every day. The energy seems to be much more stable now. Thank you so very much for your help!

Barbara, 45 years
I have been living with Kundalini for the past eight years. There have been many times that it has been a tremendously difficult, challenging and lonely journey for me. I had a premature awakening of Kundalini with no preparation and very little support and guidance in the months and years that followed after this tremendous force of life energy erupted in my body.

Since the beginning of my journey with kundalini, every aspect of my person has been substantially altered. That is to say that the energy has had a tremendous impact on my physical, mental and emotional health. In the earlier years there were a number of periods when I was very unwell, as I struggled to adapt to this enormous power of energy within my body.

I have lived for eight years with considerable pain owing to my difficulty in adapting to the energy, and the resistances that it has met within me. Because of the exceedingly difficult experience, which I had when the energy prematurely opened within me, and the ongoing pain that has followed, I have often been resentful and angry that I was chosen to live with kundalini.

This was made more difficult for me because I attributed my awakening of Kundalini to an encounter with a spiritual teacher who I did not have a trusting and healthy relationship with. This teacher confirmed to me that he had awakened the kundalini within me by means of the shaktipat touch.

Recently I sought help for myself because I was experiencing a lot of pain with the kundalini process. I came across Tara's website and organised a meeting with her by telephone.

In the work which I carried out with her over four sessions, I feel that I made very significant progress in confronting some deeply held fears within me. These fears related to my sub-conscious attachment to the spiritual teacher whom I was still in connection with at a mental level. I was also extremely uncomfortable owing to the pain I was experiencing in my body.

After working with Tara I was able to successfully detach from my unhealthy relationship with the spiritual master and take back the power that I had given to him. I found great consolation physically, mentally and emotionally when I turned fully to God, relying solely on his guidance to direct me.

Since undertaking this work with Tara, I have been a lot more comfortable since the pain in my body has significantly decreased and as my health has improved, my self-esteem has also begun to strengthen.

I also experienced a great source of inner strength from being able to share my experience of Kundalini with another person who gives genuine guidance from her own experience of this energy. This was extremely helpful because it has never been easy to talk to friends and even family about my journey with kundalini, and medics have always put my symptoms down to mental health issues, which has been further isolating.

Since I have become more accepting of the energy, I have been able to pay more attention to the subtle changes which it has been making within me. Although the process continues to be very challenging, I can acknowledge the enormous growth, which I continue to make, and I take courage in knowing that as long as I am open to the teaching of the kundalini, I am moving ever closer to God.

This helps me to be ever more at peace with myself as my greatest desire is to love and live in perfect union with God.

Michael, 34 years
"After having a completely unexpected and very powerful Kundalini awakening I was left extremely confused and at times terrified! Tara has helped me to get my feet back on the ground, not get so worked up about everything that's been happening and to actually embrace the change that I'm working through. I do Tara's higher consciousness exercise every day and it really helps – I would recommend it to everyone even without the turbulent Kundalini awakening! Thank you!"

About Tara Springett

Tara Springett M.A. holds a Masters in Education and has postgraduate psychotherapeutic qualifications in gestalt therapy, body awareness therapy and transpersonal therapy. Tara has worked as a drugs counsellor, adolescent counsellor and general psychotherapist since 1988. Since 2011 she has specialised in helping people with kundalini syndrome.

Tara has been a practising Buddhist since 1986 and has spent many weeks in solo and group retreats. In 1997 her Buddhist teacher Rigdzin Shikpo encouraged her to teach Buddhism and meditation to others. In 2002 her current teacher, His Eminence Garchen Rinpoche, asked her to teach as well.

Tara's kundalini was awakened during a year's course of intensive bio-energetic therapy in 1985. After a year of crisis and confusion, she became a Buddhist and has, ever since, experienced her kundalini as a great asset for her personal and spiritual development.

Tara lives in a retreat house in Devon, England with her soulmate and husband Nigel and their son. Tara concentrates on one-to-one work via skype and phone with people suffering from kundalini symptoms. You can contact her via her website at www.taraspringett.com/contact.

Printed in Great Britain
by Amazon